MODUS OPERANDI:
A Writer's Guide to How Criminals Work

by
Mauro V. Corvasce
Joseph R. Paglino

WRITER'S DIGEST BOOKS
Cincinnati, Ohio

The information contained in this book is intended for use in works of fiction, to add an element of accuracy. The authors and F&W Publications, Inc., cannot be held liable for the criminal use of the information herein.

 Published by Writer's Digest Books, an imprint of F&W Publications, Inc., 1507 Dana Avenue, Cincinnati, Ohio 45207. 1-800-289-0963. First edition.

99 98 97 96 95   5 4 3 2 1

Library of Congress Cataloging-in-Publication Data

Corvasce, Mauro V.
Modus operandi: a writer's guide to how criminals work / by Mauro V. Corvasce, Joseph R. Paglino.
p. cm. – (The Howdunit series)
Includes index.
ISBN 0-89879-649-0
1. Mystery and detective stories—Authorship. 2. Crime writing—Authorship. 3. Crime—Research. I. Paglino, Joseph R. II. Title. III. Series
3373.5.D4C67 1995
808'.02—dc20 94-49705
CIP

Edited by Catherine Brohaugh
Designed by Angela Lennert

Acknowledgements

First, I would like to thank my beautiful wife Elizabeth for all the assistance, cooperation and encouragement that she has given me from the very beginning.

To my two wonderful children, Kristina and Nicholas, for behaving while Mommy was typing the book and understanding why Daddy is never home.

To all those magnificent people from Novelists, Inc., too many to list here, who assisted, guided, prayed and pushed for our success.

To Richard O. Arther, the Director of the National Training Center of Polygraph Science, New York City, for enlightening me on how to use my mental tools that I didn't know I possessed.

To my boss, John Kaye, the Monmouth County Prosecutor, Freehold, New Jersey, for his consent in doing this book and the many other endeavors I have done.

To the fantastic people at F&W Publications, Bill Brohaugh for the opportunity of a lifetime, Jack Heffron for his patience and guidance, and Catherine Brohaugh for a job well done.

To our agent Steven Axelrod of the Axelrod Agency, Lenox, Massachusetts, for representing two newcomers.

To all the people who affected my life in a positive way.

—Mauro V. Corvasce

To Bill Brohaugh, for having the trust and confidence in us to author this work.

To Prosecutor John Kaye, Monmouth County Prosecutor's Office, New Jersey, for his professional support in our endeavors.

To all the warm, sincere and helpful members of Novelists, Inc., including JoAnn Ross, Laura Taylor and Rebecca Brandywyne for their positive and undying support from the beginning of it all.

To Michelle, Christopher and Danielle, my family, for the patience of being accustomed to the long and odd hours of police work and this project.

—Joseph R. Paglino

Table of Contents

Introduction

Modus Operandi, or method of operation, is really a term that refers to the habits, techniques and peculiarities of behavior of a criminal. All criminals have a modus operandi, and enough of them have distinctive methods of operation to justify the classification of crimes by like characteristics. The modus operandi of a criminal is his "signature."

Law enforcement agencies maintain modus operandi files which enable detectives to recognize a pattern of criminal behavior, to associate a group of crimes with a single perpetrator, to predict approximately the next target of the criminal and the next time he will strike, and to assist complainants, eyewitnesses and detectives in recognizing the perpetrator through recorded characteristics of the criminal activity. The modus operandi file is most effective in personal contact crimes such as felonies against the person, confidence schemes and burglaries.

The traditional method of compiling a modus operandi file is still considered effective after forty years of use. In this system the following are considered important elements in the effectiveness of such a file.

1. *Property*—the type of stolen property provides an excellent clue in larceny or burglary crimes.
2. *Description*—if the criminal was observed, a verbal description is usually the most important clue to the identity of the perpetrator. If the person has been arrested before, the file will also contain a mug shot.
3. *Observation at the Scene*—the use of all senses at the scene of a crime is important because it may result in finding a useful pattern. The objects and substances seen, heard, smelled, tasted or felt will contribute to the complete picture.
4. *Motive*—in addition to the taking of property, there are many other criminal motives. Occasionally, such as in murder, rape or assault in general, a pattern of behavior may be seen in a series of crimes. This pattern

is particularly common in crimes committed by a psychopath.

5. *Time*—the time at which the crimes were committed is an important element in the pattern. Naturally, since the exact moment of occurrence cannot be readily established in many cases, the detective must try to establish the time of occurrence within reasonable limits.
6. *Peculiarities*—weaknesses of character will ordinarily reveal themselves in the unaltered surrounds of the crime. Peculiarities such as drinking a victim's liquor or eating a victim's food, defecation at the scene or a particular location, and theft of items that seem unimportant, such as ties or cufflinks, are significant.
7. *Observed Peculiarities*—an observer of the offense may be able to supply valuable clues by noting the criminal's idiosyncrasies. Speech patterns, a lisp or an accent are important clues to identity. Also, enunciation, dialect and diction can be recorded.

Detectives compare the way in which a crime was committed with records stored in the modus operandi section of police records. If these comparisons are successful, a detective obtains data on possible suspects. Detectives also report the modus operandi to other detectives at monthly meetings to make comparisons. Police agencies use modus operandi files extensively; they are very successful in solving burglary, robbery, grand theft, fraud, sex and fraudulent checks crimes.

The modus operandi file contains so much information about the method of operations of known criminals that it often reads like a biography. These files can identify a perpetrator by naming suspects whose modus operandi in past crimes fits the facts of the current crimes. Of course, a suspect's past crimes and operations must be sufficiently similar to be identified. They must have several features in common with the crime under investigation to warrant making a connection between the two.

Similarities in methods of operation, in combination with other leads, are important tools in identifying criminals, for they decrease the likelihood of a mistake in suspecting a person of a crime. Storing data on crimes according to modus operandi allows police to compare unsolved crimes with the criminal technique of an apprehended criminal. Connecting these unsolved crimes to an arrested person means the police must continually update their modus operandi files; otherwise pertinent criminal activity may be missed.

Here is an example of how modus operandi works: While working as a detective for the Brooklyn District Attorney's Office, Joe had investigated a series of home burglaries that occurred in Brooklyn. During the course of these burglaries, the thief would defecate on the kitchen table no matter what time of the day or night he struck the unoccupied home. In some instances, defecation is used as revenge against a particular person. However, in this particular thief's M.O., he would always defecate *in a particular location*—the victim's kitchen table.

A man named Nick was recently released from prison and had started to burglarize homes in the area. While Nick was incarcerated, he learned the tricks of his trade even better. After all, consider jail a kind of college where you learn your trade better than if you were out in the cold, cruel world and had to work for a living. Nick learned how to pop open windows better, how to jimmy the garage door better, and how to bypass the alarm better. He also learned how to select his victims, so he would get bigger and better takes of merchandise in the same amount of time. But one thing Nick did not learn was a new modus operandi: After breaking into a home through his usual methods, which happened to be through a patio door or rear window, and always starting at the rear of the home, then he would defecate on the victim's kitchen table. He did this for one reason: He was nervous! His criminal activity created such a turmoil in his body that he actually had to move his bowels.

Now, why did he choose the kitchen table? The real reason was because he was obsessive-compulsive about germs—he constantly washed his hands and was constantly concerned about getting sick from germs. While he was incarcerated, he was known to take piles of toilet paper, magazines, books, paper towels or whatever he could and place them on the seat of the toilet so that his bare skin did not actually touch it. Also, he didn't like to flush the toilet with his hand on the handle, so he would use a disposable object, such as a stick. He would not even stoop to flushing the toilet using his shoe, because that would make germs on the bottom of his shoe which could possibly spread to his body.

In the early stages of these home burglaries, Joe noted that Nick would frequently defecate in the person's bathroom, and the detectives would find the toilet seat layered with many, many pieces of toilet paper. Coincidentally, Nick did catch an infection in his genital area. He attributed this to using the victim's toilet, although it was not a possibility because of the toilet paper placed on the seat. So from that point on, he simply defecated on the victim's kitchen table.

When this particular M.O. showed up, Joe simply went to Nick and casually confronted him. During a casual, approved search, to which Nick consented, the criminal's home was found to contain many items that were linked to the burglaries which had occurred weeks and months earlier in Brooklyn. This is a classic case of a criminal's method of operation leading the police to his capture.

In this book, you will learn how and why criminals operate. Their modi operandi, which, until now, were clandestine and known only to themselves and the police departments investigating them, are now known to you. So, let us step into the shoes of the criminals who operate day or night and learn the tricks of their trade. Be forewarned—the experience can be arresting!

O N E

ARSONISTS

Arson is the most underreported of all crimes because evidence that could be left behind is usually destroyed by the fire. Fire investigators are trained to determine the *origin* (where the fire started) and the *cause* (what started the fire). If an arsonist performs his craft perfectly, the fire investigator will find it extremely difficult to determine the origin and the cause of the fire.

Amateur arsonists attempt to fool the fire investigator by placing a flammable or combustible material in or near an electrical outlet. The arsonist thinks that the investigator will see the *burn pattern* (the direction that the fire burns, also known as the *V pattern*) at the electrical outlet and determine that the fire started through faulty wiring or electrical devices in the building. However, a trained fire investigator knows that for an electrical short to start a fire, certain other elements must be present.

These elements are a fuel source, an oxygen source, an ignition source or heat, and an uninhibited chemical reaction among the three. This is known as the fire triangle.

1. Fuel can be any type of flammable or combustible material—solid, liquid or a vapor.
2. An oxygen source is necessary so the fire can "breathe" and maintain a strong, steady rate of burn.
3. An ignition or heat source could be the striking of a match by the hands of an arsonist or an electrical malfunction which causes overheating and/or a spark.
4. The uninhibited chemical reaction is the above three elements—the fire triangle—coming together to start a fire.

The trained fire investigator must evaluate these four elements in deciding whether or not the cause of the fire is accidental or arson. By comparing these elements with other factors, the cause can be properly determined. For example, in dealing with the electrical short circuit, some factors, such as the wire beading up, or forming small balls of melted metal at the point of the short, or *sleeving*, the loosening of the insulation from the wire, will indicate arson or a malfunction. Also, a circuit breaker will "trip" off when the wire is overloaded. These are the tell-tale signs that an arson investigator will use to make his determination.

To incorporate arsonists in whodunits, the writer must first understand the legal definition of arson. A person is guilty of arson if he or she starts a fire or causes an explosion whether on his property or another. Arson is covered in the law by degrees, which accommodate different intents of the arsonists, such as causing death or bodily injury to a person or collecting insurance for destruction or damage to the property.

Cause

There are two types of fire causes. The first is accidental. An accidental fire is caused either by someone's carelessness or by equipment malfunction.

The second fire cause is the incendiary fire. This fire is started on purpose by an individual with the intent of destruction. An incendiary fire may have indications of multiple fire origins, and a flammable or combustible material used to start the fire may also be found. There may be few, if any, contents remaining in the building, but valuable or irreplaceable items, such as photographs, insurance papers or money, will not be recovered, as the arsonist may steal such items thinking they will be presumed lost in the fire rather than stolen.

Origin

Origin and cause are closely related. When considering using arson and fire investigators as part of your plot, keep the following rules of fire in mind:

1. The cause of the fire will be found at the point of origin.
2. The fire will burn longer at the point of origin than at other places to which the fire has spread.
3. If any flammable or combustible materials were used to ignite the fire, a sample should be found at the point of origin.
4. The fire will spread from the point of origin to the rest of the building (this is known as the *direction of fire travel*).
5. Determining the point of origin will either confirm or refute the stories of the principals involved.

Obviously, there are many ways to start a fire. Here are some of the most common, along with other attendant terminology.

Dynamite is basically used to blow up an object, but it could be used in conjunction with another fuel source, such as gasoline, to create not only a blast but a fireball that would spread the fire quickly. Sticks of dynamite are short and fat or long and thin. They are stamped with a product name (gelatin dynamite), a date-shipped code, and the manufacturer's name.

Cast boosters are small and stronger than dynamite. When detonated, cast boosters look like soda cans. These explosives are used to increase or support other explosives, and they can be used like dynamite to spread the fire faster. They are stamped with the product name, size, weight, and a date-shipped code.

An Electronic Detonator or Blasting Cap is an aluminum-shelled primer—a smaller explosive used to ignite a larger blasting agent—about the size of a small rifle cartridge. This aluminum shell has two wires at one end. The aluminum shell is placed into the explosive, either dynamite or plastic, to begin a chain reaction once the primer is set off. The wires exiting the aluminum shell of the primer are attached to a pair of electrical wires and then to a detonating device.

Black powder is basically gun powder, similar to what was used in single-shot muzzle-loading rifles and pistols. It can be compressed in a container to cause an explosion. These containers become pipe bombs. Black powder can also be used to refill inert fragmentation grenades which can be purchased through military surplus stores.

Cartridge count is the total strength of an explosive composed of the explosive's weight, density and strength.

Detonation occurs in three ways: manual (lighting a fuse), electric/electronic (sending a current), or mechanical (pulling a pin out of a grenade).

Military explosives are compact, waterproof and olive-drab, shipped in cardboard containers or coated by a Mylar film package.

Commercial explosives are more brightly decorated than military explosives, stamped with a description of use, and safety warnings.

Primacord (also referred to as detonating cord) is a spool of multicolored fabric-covered wire. Inside the fabric covering is a high explosive used to send a detonating wave. If you wrapped the cord around a tree and detonated it, the tree would bc cut in half where the cord rested. Primacord is utilized by the military to quickly clear LZs (landing zones) or to cut through bridge supports.

A delay mechanism can be either an electrical, chemical, or mechanical time-delay element. This device can be used alone or in combination with others. It could be as simple as a burning cigarette resting on a book of matches or a wristwatch wired so that when the hands come together an electric circuit is completed.

Incendiary material burns with a very hot flame for a certain period of time and is used to set fire to other material and eventually the structure itself. These materials need not be sophisticated or scientific; they could be as simple as a cigarette.

Automobile and Other Vehicle Arson

Automobiles *seem* to be very combustible. As you are quite aware, they contain flammable liquids, have many electrical circuits, and their interiors are made of combustible material. Combine that with a careless smoker and you have a vehicle fire, or so you would think. But actually, with new technology, most interiors are fire resistant – a cigarette will seldom ignite a seat cover or floor mat, the fuel systems are designed with safety in mind, and the electrical circuits arc shut off by fuses and other interrupt devices.

Accidental vehicle fires do occur, but the fire generally remains in one compartment, i.e. engine, trunk, glove compartment or interior. As with all things, an accidental vehicle fire can also engulf the entire vehicle. Mauro investigated one such occurrence when a teenager, who decided he could make it home with a flat tire, drove home on the rim. He did not realize the rim was a magnesium alloy, and the friction of driving started a fire of unbelievable temperature, which consumed the vehicle in a short time.

There are two types of vehicle arsonists: amateur and professional. An amateur is usually behind on his car payments and desperate to rid himself of the car. He knows that the vehicle must be declared totaled by his insurance company, so he will go for mass destruction. The professional is not necessarily a professional arsonist but a professional criminal who uses vehicle arson to conceal other crimes: stolen cars used during the commission of a crime, or a homicide, for example.

In general, after driving the car to a remote location, the arsonist will completely dowse the interior and exterior of the vehicle with a combustible material such as gasoline or lighter fluid and set the fire. A one- to five-gallon gas can is generally found at the scene. Using five gallons is quite dangerous, and the arsonist may end up like the car because of the flammable vapors that have saturated the area.

The arsonist might make what are known as *trailers* by pouring a stream of gasoline from the vehicle to a location he feels is far enough away from the vehicle to ignite it safely. These types of fires are easily tagged as arsons because of the evidence left behind. Sometimes, the fire will be started by a road flare, which can easily be thrown from a safe distance into the vehicle.

Vehicle fires for profit or to mask a crime are not limited to automobiles. Small trucks, large trucks, buses, vans, planes and boats all could be set ablaze in the manner described above. The bigger, more exotic vehicles, such as airplanes could be equipped to blow up or ignite while flying. This is done so that a crash appears to be caused by mechanical problems rather than caused deliberately.

In vehicle fires when the insurance money is important, the fire will be started in or near the engine compartment to make it look like an equipment malfunction. If it is to cover up an additional crime or evidence, the whole vehicle will be set ablaze with a flammable substance. The same is true with boats and planes. Often the fire is started from a trailer.

We can all remember the tragic bombing of the airliner over Lockerby, Scotland, which killed all passengers. The incendiary device was placed in a small AM/FM cassette-radio brought onto the plane through a series of elaborate cargo shipping procedures. The radio was placed on one plane in a nonterrorist stronghold where security procedures were weak and did not detect it. Once aboard the plane, the radio was placed with the other cargo, and through either altitude or time delay, the explosives were set off. The small amount of explosives that the radio contained was enough to create a small hole causing the plane to crash.

Arson for Hire

Arson for hire generally involves structure fires. A person owns a building, and for financial reasons, decides it's time to bail out. The owner needs to find an arsonist. He seeks out someone who he feels may be willing to participate in the scheme—he may approach a trusted employee or contact a network of shady characters. A secret meeting is set up with the arsonist.

At the meeting, the professional arsonist will ask for plans of the building, which include sprinkler and alarm systems, types of locks, and hidden, dimly lit points of entry. If there are no secluded entry points, a light may be intentionally left off, so no one can see the arsonist enter the building.

The arsonist usually gives a list of instructions to the building owner to prepare for the arson. In the weeks or days before the fire, the owner will set off false alarms, indicating a problem with the system. This will give him cause not to set the alarm system the evening of the arson.

Another instruction will be to disable the sprinkler system. Sprinkler systems, especially in large buildings, have emergency shut off valves in case of accidental set offs. Most of the time, they are located on an exterior wall or on the lawn adjacent to the building itself. These valves are secured by a chain and padlock. The chain is easily cut with a bolt cutter and the valves closed. This way the fire will not be suppressed or slowed by the sprinklers.

Other instructions to the building owner include materials the arsonist may need to accelerate the spread of the fire. For example, placing a number of flammable liquids used in the manufacturing process of the company in key locations to spread the fire throughout the building.

Once the arsonist is ready, he will tell the building owner that now is the time to develop a credible alibi and may suggest a weekend trip to the Bahamas.

The arsonist usually sets the fire in the early morning hours for various reasons: less chance of detection because the factory will be closed and traffic will be light on the street, the fire will burn longer before it is discovered, and no workers will be in the building, so loss of lives will be avoided.

The arsonist may or may not break into the building. He may use a key to gain entry or a door will be left unlocked. Once inside, he uses available combustibles along with a device to ensure ignition after his exit from the scene.

Some arsonists may even set up obstacles or devices that will deter the suppression of the fire. These devices could be as simple as chaining fences that the firefighter has to take time to cut open, or positioning chemicals that, when touched by the water used in suppression of the fire, react violently and cause the fire to become hotter and burn faster.

Pyromaniacs

Pyromaniacs are the most complex type of arsonist. They often set large destructive fires with no thought of the consequences. It is believed they enjoy a sort of sexual gratification from starting fires. Their fires are well thought out, almost as well as those of the arsonist for hire, but the pyromaniac will make all the arrangements for lighting the fire himself. He will study the layout of the building, determine how to disconnect sprinkler and alarm systems, and set traps, not only to slow the firefighters, but to actually hurt them. He will use devices that will make the fire spread quickly and violently. His only intent is to destroy. Pyromaniacs are the most dangerous arsonists and the hardest to catch.

Let's walk through a scenario. The arsonist goes to a warehouse district during the daytime hours to scout some possible targets. Once he locates a target, he returns that night to perform additional scouting without detection. He may even, if the building is unoccupied at the time, break into the building to determine if there are enough materials on hand to start and sustain a fire. Once this preplanning is finished, he will carry out his plans.

He returns during the evening hours and places gallon plastic milk containers filled with alcohol throughout the building. He connects these gallon containers with trailers, usually rags soaked in alcohol. He lights the trailers, which will carry the flame throughout the building. He exits the building and may leave altogether or stay in the neighborhood to watch the building burn. Some pyromaniacs only get a kick out of lighting the fire.

Firestarters

Persons who start fires do so for a number of reasons. These reasons may be to seek fame, to get even, personal finance, rage or curiosity. These next few profiles will give the writer some information as to how and for what reasons people start fires.

The Hero

Security guards and volunteer firefighters are generally in good positions to start fires. These types of firesetters are attention-seekers or would-be heroes. For example, a security guard working the morning tour of duty ignites a small, controllable fire such as a pile of debris or a trash can. He "discovers" the fire and gives the alarm to save the building. He becomes a hero. Or, a volunteer firefighter sets a controllable, nonlethal fire in a garbage dumpster or small shed. He does this by using materials located at the scene and igniting them. Both the security guard and the firefighter will experiment and eventually branch out to abandoned buildings, and then to occupied buildings, in an attempt to become bigger and better heroes, perhaps even saving someone's life.

These types of fires are usually a spur of the moment decision. Excessive alcohol consumption has been related to these firestarters.

A third type of hero firestarters are police-buff arsonists. Police-buff arsonists are just like the security guards and volunteer firefighter arsonists in that they are attempting to win praise and social recognition and are usually at the scene giving assistance to the authorities. They will light fires at a location such as a home for people with special needs or people who are nonambulatory. They pick these locations because they will get the most sympathy and attention for helping fight the fire.

The Lover

Some arsonists act from vanity and jealous rage. Men tend to set fire to the vehicle or home of a current or former lover to get even with her. His goal is to create large, dangerous fires with the intent of total destruction. He brings flammable and combustible materials to the scene knowing what will happen after igniting them. The apartment building or house itself will be set afire from materials on hand with matches and a lighter. These types of fires are often set late at night, after a heavy drinking binge or a violent argument.

Women, on the other hand, light very small fires, usually on the bed using materials on hand such as facial tissues or the man's clothing. She will make a small combustible pile and set it on fire using matches or a lighter.

The Juvenile

Juvenile firesetters are complex and bewildering to investigate. One may light a fire by playing with matches out of curiosity, or it could be a vengeful or hostile action with the intent of destroying property and life. Most of the time, juvenile firestarters plan the fire well and use materials at the scene and flammable liquids.

Juvenile firestarters are sometimes caught by their own experimentation. In one case, a boy would sit around and watch the flame of his small disposable lighter. One day, the lighter overheated, causing a small explosion. The boy later died from the injuries he received when the lighter exploded and ignited his clothing.

As the juvenile firesetter reaches his teen years, he collects fire tools such as a box of wooden matches and small bottles filled with flammable liquids to experiment with fire bombs. He may even make small pipe bombs by compressing match heads into a pipe. The pipe can be half-inch diameter copper pipe with the ends folded over. The pipe is then thrown into a small fire. The firestarter will sit around to watch it explode. This is very dangerous because the match heads can explode while they are being packed into the pipe.

Eventually, either by themselves or in small groups, they set an abandoned building on fire using combustible materials such as pieces of furniture, bed coverings or curtains. They pile these materials throughout the building, light the piles, and exit running. These building are usually close to their own homes, so they wait at home until the fire trucks arrive, then return to the scene to watch the fire.

The Others

Other arsonists may act alone or with a close friend. Like most firestarters, he will work in darkness to prevent apprehension and to sneak around undetected. He studies the layout of the building, either through remote surveillance or at the scene. He carries a small amount of flammable liquid, approaches the house from a side where he can conceal his actions, splashes or pours the flammable liquid on an outside wall of the building, and ignites it.

This type of fire, even though extremely dangerous, takes more time to start. This delay gives the arsonist enough time to return to his car and drive past as if he were going for a midnight ride. He jumps out to save the day and assists with the evacuation of the building to the extent of suffering injury including smoke inhalation. This type of behavior will happen again and again until he is apprehended. The difference between the "hero" and this arsonist is the former is seeking attention while the latter is just looking for something to do.

Typical Arson Scenarios

A restaurant is no longer turning a profit and property values in the area are down. The owners decide to recoup their investment through the insurance company. The restaurant is entered during the early morning hours. The doors are pried open and the office is ransacked, a safe may be broken into or removed to indicate a burglary. A flammable liquid is poured on the floor and trailers may be used. Pots or other containers found in the restaurant are used to hold additional flammable liquid. This procedure is continued throughout the building and the arsonists leave some type of delayed fuse mechanism, perhaps a twenty-minute burning candle at the base of a cup filled with alcohol. Another possible time-delay mechanism is a coffeemaker filled with flammable liquids set for a particular time. These mechanisms allow the restaurant owners to exit and get some distance away before the discovery of the fire.

Two burglars realize that their elderly victims have awakened and observed them as they are trying to exit the house. Knowing the elderly couple can identify them as neighborhood kids, the burglars attack and eventually kill the couple. In an attempt to conceal the homicides, they put the couple back in bed and set fire to the bed using material on hand in an attempt to make it look like an accidental smoking-in-bed fire.

A local gang demands pay up money from a local merchant. The merchant refuses to comply with their demands, so the gang decides that it's time to teach him a lesson. Early one morning, a few of the gang members assemble with a homemade napalm-type bomb—bottles filled with gasoline and soap and a fuse made of cloth stuck into the neck of the bottle. They walk or drive by the front of the store, light the cloth fuses, and throw the bottles through the window causing a fair amount of damage.

Some Final Thoughts on Arson

One thing to remember is that the professional arsonist mainly uses items to start, spread, and sustain the fire that are readily found in the building itself. He does not want to draw undue attention to himself by carrying five-gallon gas cans around. The arsonist also has to assume that if the fire is detected early and suppressed, any evidence he left will make a second attempt more difficult. It may even lead to his arrest.

The amateur uses large amounts of flammable liquid to start the fire and combustible materials to spread the fire. He starts the fire without a delay mechanism, usually by open flame. In the process, he may even burn himself.

In dealing with arson, we rarely come across any type of explosive devices. Explosives are usually used just to get the fire going, but if the building is big enough, there may be a number of ignition devices found scattered throughout the property.

For those of you who may be uncertain about what types of flammable liquids are used, they mainly range from gasoline to lighter fluid and alcohol. The storage area of a bar will be used to fuel the fire's growth by starting a fire underneath or near the liquor supply.

Trailer material can be the flammable liquid itself poured in a line on the ground. It could also be cloth or paper soaked in a flammable liquid or a series of small fires or anything else that would cause the fire to spread throughout the building.

T W O

Art, Antique and Jewel Thieves

When we discuss art these days, we're talking about a business of far-reaching proportions. Art prices have skyrocketed because art is now viewed as a more stable and profitable investment than stocks, bonds or mutual funds. Owning artwork has a uniqueness that other types of investments may lack. For some, an art collection, whether Grandma's silver spoons or a van Gogh, is a more intimate part of a person's life and lifestyle than actual money can ever be. Art therefore has a dual grip on a person: its value as an investment and its aesthetic impact. When these types of objects are stolen, they are often deemed irreplaceable.

There are three main reasons art and jewelry thefts occur: to get the money from fencing stolen art; a collector personally safekeeps art as it increases in value; or, for political, or possibly sociopolitical reasons—sometimes considered terrorism. Just before the 1994 Winter Olympics in

Keep In Mind . . .

It seems no matter how hard the police work, thefts of art, jewelry and antiques continue. Before the 1950s, art, jewelry and precious antiques did not appreciate in value as rapidly as they have within the last thirty-five to forty years. Keep this in mind if your art and jewelry theft story is set in a historical period. Although mankind has continually produced works of art for over 40,000 years, art did not become generally perceived as a commodity, or as a means of economic exchange, until 150 to 200 years ago. A novel that is set in historical times will, of course, have its period antiques and artwork that are valuable. However, the appreciation value will not be as great as it has been in the last thirty-five to forty years.

Norway, Edvard Munch's *The Scream* was stolen by abortion protesters in an attempt to negotiate political policy through terrorism.

One of the most famous politically motivated art thefts of the twentieth century occurred at the Louvre in 1911 when an Italian house painter stole the *Mona Lisa* from the wall where it hung. The *Mona Lisa* disappeared for approximately two years. When the thief finally gave himself up, he claimed that he had only stolen it for political reasons, and that he had intended to take the painting back to Florence, Italy, where da Vinci had painted it, and where he felt it rightfully belonged.

Types of Art Theft

The past thirty-five to forty years have seen an unprecedented boom in organized art robbery running parallel to an equally unprecedented boom in the legitimate art market. To a degree, the thieves help the legitimate dealers, whether the latter know it or not, because the art market depends on a pool of homeless works of art fed at one end by the sale of objects, drained at the other by the forming of new collections. In the last fifty years that pool has been increasingly agitated. The turnover of works of art through auction rooms and dealers has accelerated year by year. At the same time, the quantity of available works of art by dead artists is reduced: either through accidents or through acquisition of this or that Rembrandt by a museum.

It would sensationalize the problem to suggest that the art market, especially during the 1970s, was heavily dependent on recirculating stolen objects. The proportion is higher in the field of simple works of art such as silverware, furniture, drawings, rare prints, engravings, porcelain and antiquities, than in the area of signed paintings by acknowledged, famous artists. Not only are there more of the former around, but their histories are infinitely harder to check and the records of their existence, if there are any, are more difficult to obtain.

Archaeological Antiquities

Thousands of objects are smuggled yearly from countries rich in antiquities to countries rich in economy. This is a particular problem for archaeological artifacts. Many millions of dollars worth of art are steadily being stolen from archaeological sites. Once an object is removed from its original site, the archaeologist has lost a valuable clue to interpreting a culture. The enormous profitability of acquiring or smuggling antiquities has led to the depletion of cultural treasures in many countries.

Popular Culture

Thieves don't always need high art to make a killing. Let's take for example, the recent rise in the popularity of dinosaurs. Let's face it—dinosaurs are hot! No need to remind you of one of the biggest box office hits of late, *Jurassic Park*. Along with *Jurassic Park*, came millions of dollars in T-shirts, sweatshirts, memorabilia, movies, prints and novel sales. When you discuss art and jewelry thefts, you must include other historically significant and desirable commodities. And what do you think were some of the hottest items stolen during the dinosaur revolution of the last five years? Archaeological findings and prehistoric memorabilia; actual artifacts and dinosaur bones, fossilized dinosaur eggs, imprints of dinosaur footprints, anything to do with dinosaurs. It was a hot commodity, and the prices skyrocketed.

Organized Crime

Organized criminal elements are turning their attention to the art world. Organized crime has always been quick to exploit the trends originally set by legitimate businesses such as alcohol vendors. In this case, the master criminal becomes aware of the enormous profit potential of art and begins to educate and prepare himself for this particular field. Additionally, just as financial consultants have established mutual funds and invested solely in works of art, so the criminal is now beginning to appreciate the investment value of art. In fact, even when recoveries are made, the frequent absence of one or two of the best pieces suggests stockpiling by the criminal element.

Crime bosses and small-time crooks began to buy museum catalogs and art magazines and look very hard at the old and new masters. Compared to burglary or bank robbery, art thefts are easy and pay well for little risk. Many museums, prior to the 1960s, had never heard of security alarms, let alone used them. Insurance companies and owners who wanted the unique treasures returned safely would not argue about rewards or ransoms.

So the crime bosses began to convert their henchmen into art thieves. When they found the extortion racket worked, they invented others: dealing stolen religious objects, altering them and filtering them into an antique market; new techniques in art smuggling; and selling novel art forms such as Hong Kong Ming. An equally inspiring tale of boldness was when a criminal sold Salvatore Dali one of his own stolen paintings. Remember that criminals play on human frailty and sorrow, and the fact that every man believes himself to be something of a discoverer and cannot resist the lure of easy money. The attempt by a person to make quick and easy money is one of the greatest human instincts.

Forgeries

A unique example of cultural and artistic work exists in parts of Africa. Much African art is carved in traditional styles, artificially aged, and then sold under false pretenses. These forgeries are so well executed, only the most competent experts are able to detect them. East African carvers visit museums to study the aging process and style of art objects. In Nigeria, West Africa, carvers generally have better access to museums than in the East, and are able to familiarize themselves with the art market.

Art Theft to Order

Remember that the art and antique thief does not have to be the person who physically removes the item from the home, business or museum. The actual thief, in terms of the police investigation, would not only be the person who physically removed the item, but the person who set the wheels in motion.

For example: We have Mr. Jones, a collector of fine art and antiques. He's collected nearly all the signed original works of Salvatore Dali created during a certain time period when Dali, let's say, was at a certain level of impressionism in his painting. Mr. Jones does not have one painting and desires that one very much.

We must remember that artists have periods in their lives, much like musicians, when their art takes on a certain style somewhat different from years before and the years that follow. So this collector, Mr. Jones, simply must have the one missing painting. He hires a private detective firm to find the rightful owner of the painting. But, the rightful owner is determined not to sell. If he still wants the painting, Mr. Jones must decide to do one of two things:

Scenario 1: He may decide to have another person (a broker) approach the owner on his behalf for the sale of the painting. Of course, this is risky because, if the painting is stolen shortly after the person turns down the offer, the owner would only have to alert the local authorities as to who contacted him. However, should the broker approach the rightful owner and not represent exactly who he is trying to buy it for, then it cannot be traced as easily. Another downfall to this type of bid is that the owner will probably sell it to Mr. Jones at top dollar.

Scenario 2: Now let's proceed to the more common way of acquiring the desired painting. Mr. Jones will use the services of a quasi-legal private investigator to determine the rightful owner and location of the desired painting. From that point he contacts a fence who he knows will deal in stolen art and antiques. Of course, these fences are sub-specialists to regular fences and are extremely difficult to find unless you know how. In these incidents the art, antique and jewelry fence will not be your corner pawnbroker, but may in fact be another legitimate dealer or an avid collector of these works.

After reaching out to the professional art fence, it is the fence's turn to go into action as a broker. The fence contracts to someone else for the physical theft. In this particular instance the object is stolen to order.

In It for the Money

Mr. Jones wanted the missing Dali for personal pleasure. Now, the professional art thief has a completely different set of rules. Although any work of art in theory can be stolen, its usefulness to a thief depends on a complex web of interplaying factors. What is the demand on the free market for the item? How anonymous is the work of art or how can its identity be removed without destroying its value? Is it likely to be cataloged or recorded? Two principles determine the criminal's final choice: If it is not desirable it will not sell; if it is well known it can be traced.

The Role of the Fence in Art Theft

In the case of art, jewelry and antique thefts, the fence plays a crucial and pivotal role in the theft process. A fence, of course, is a person who will actually receive the property from the thief, and then either use it for his own benefit, or turn around and sell it to someone interested in the commodity, who in turn may resell it. You can imagine how difficult it is to get rid of something that is significant historically and politically, especially immediately after the crime has been committed. That is why in most of the cases where there is a major art or jewelry theft, everything has already been laid in place for the ultimate disposal of that stolen item.

For example, let's assume there is a family who is very wealthy and has collected several Salvador Dalí paintings. The home is burglarized, but the wheels were set in motion weeks to months before for the ultimate disposal of those paintings. The theft of them will make the local and, sometimes, national newspapers, but by that time, the items will have already been deposited with their new owner. In this manner, the fence is acting more in the capacity of a broker, much like one for stocks or bonds. The art and jewelry thief must use the fence to dispose of the item in advance, because of its uniqueness and difficulty of disposing it through routine channels.

Follow along the progression of a theft to its ultimate disposal. Let's take the case of a very famous stamp collector. He has the stamp series issued in 1919 honoring airplanes in the United States. One stamp was accidently minted upside down and 1,000 pieces were issued. Even though many people recognized this to be collectible back in 1919, let's presume that 100 to 150 of the stamps were used and postmarked by the Post Office.

So now we have 850 uncirculated stamps grabbed up by collectors back in 1919. Be aware of the fact that every person who collected the stamp back in 1919 has most likely either kept it, sold it or had it stolen since the date it was struck. People who collect stamps and have antique and extremely valuable collections usually know who has the missing items they need for their collection. People involved in art and antique collecting buy several items that they can use as leverage to obtain the item that they really want. Most collectors would never dream of stealing from other collectors; part of the fun for them is the bargaining and trading. But, there are people who are so engrossed in completing their collection that they will do anything to obtain the missing piece or pieces.

Capturing Art and Jewelry Thieves

Art theft and crooked fences alone keep many police forces throughout the world occupied. More than $200 million in art objects are stolen every year, making such thefts the biggest criminal pursuits after international smuggling and selling of drugs like heroin and cocaine. To combat this epidemic of art crime, police in Europe and America have set up special art theft squads.

The Art Squad

Penalties for art crimes are much stiffer in England than in the United States. In England, art theft is taken very seriously, and the minimum sentence is usually five years. The English feel that when art is stolen, part of the national heritage is also stolen. In the United States, however, jail sentences for art-related crimes are usually the exception, rather than the rule.

London is a clearinghouse for black market art and antiques, but it has one of the most efficient art detective units in the world. The Art Squad was established in 1968 at New Scotland Yard with approximately eleven detectives, and it has recovered more than $350 million dollars worth of stolen art. Among the first to use a computer, Scotland Yard has built up an international log of some 25,000 paintings and sculptures and other art treasures—a sort of identification kit. The description of artworks is fed into a mainframe computer, and within seconds, Scotland Yard can track an item offered for sale to an auction house or recovered by police forces throughout the world.

Whenever an art loss is reported, details of the stolen pieces are published in the top art and antiques magazines. This helps to stop the sale of the object on the open market since legitimate dealers resent the intrusion of illegitimate dealers into the art market. In addition, the art squad has encouraged dealers to organize and communicate. For example, if Dealer A suffers a loss, he would contact Dealers B and C, who in turn contact two more and so on. It is hoped that the publicity would keep the theft from progressing into a sale.

Members of the New Scotland Yard Art Squad are a certain breed. Not only do they know the foremost in detection methods and how to capture criminals, but they also bring a commitment to art and its heritage. Many members have a particular interest of their own, such as paintings or sculpture, furniture, silver, glass or antiques. They bring the perspective of collectors to the squad, which is invaluable.

Art and Jewelry Theft Bureau of NYC

The New York City Police Department is also active in catching art thieves with its undercover Art and Jewelry Theft Bureau. Since New York and London are key financial centers in the international art market, it is imperative that New York City occupy this position in the capture of art thieves. One of the most famous art theft detectives ever assigned to the Theft Bureau was Robert Volpe. Volpe is an artist as well as a detective, and it is this commitment to the art world that enabled Volpe to infiltrate many major art thefts rings. He was instrumental in recovering millions of dollars worth of art and jewelry and precious antiques, sculpture and the likes from the rings of thieves who attempted to sell it. Detective Volpe is one of the new breed of police officers who have become more and more specialized in areas of detective work.

Interpol

Detectives trained in the art market and experienced in the methods of dealers and crime syndicates specializing in art robberies have linked their efforts to beat the international racket. Interpol headquarters, located just outside Paris, receives dozens of reports of stolen paintings, sculptures and other rare objects and immediately circulates them to offices throughout the world. These bulletins go down the line to regional police forces who then check with their informants and contacts in the art trade. More than in any other criminal investigation, speed is vital in disseminating this information and publicizing it in the press and on television. Most stolen art sells more easily outside its country of origin, where it goes unrecognized. But once a stolen masterpiece or a valuable object appears in the press, on television or in trade publications, no honest dealer will touch it, and even the most crooked fence handles it with extreme care.

Interpol reinforces its weekly bulletin with a monthly sheet listing the twelve most wanted works of art with pictures, descriptions, and details of their theft. This international organization of police covers most of the world. Its offices around the world are staffed by local detectives who act as liaisons between Interpol and forces like the New York City Police Department, Scotland Yard, and the F.B.I. If it were not for the actions of Interpol, hundreds of paintings smuggled across borders would have vanished forever due to their international appeal.

Avoiding Capture

Much stolen art goes underground for many years until it has established a new sales pedigree and everyone has forgotten about the theft. Then it can reappear in the hands of a private dealer or even in an auction room for a legitimate sale.

Big crime bosses place stolen objects in a bank vault until the country's statute of limitations runs out and precludes their prosecution. They can then offer the painting even to its original owner for much more than it would fetch on the black market and often the painting or other art object has doubled its value during its storage.

Criminal Penalties for Art Theft

On both the national and international levels, there are few legal precedents and little legislation for dealing with art crime. For some reason, the penalties for art crime, especially in the United States, have been very light. Art and jewelry theft is close to a white collar crime, since no one was physically injured. Public opinion is ambivalent toward the matter because the general public doesn't have the means to deal in art, antique and jewelry collections, so, its theft does not affect them.

If the theft involves two different countries, e.g., the thieves steal art from France and take it to Holland, Holland may decide not to investigate. In other words, what is unpardonable to one government may not even be criminal to another. Despite the ambiguous opinions some governments and police agencies have on this subject, there seems to be relative agreement on one point: theft and vandalism, no matter what the target, constitute a criminal act, but the penalties for art and jewelry thefts are usually very light.

Conclusion

Art crime is changing from a romantic Robin Hood affair, often committed with an artistic flair, to a cold and impersonal act committed purely for money and sometimes with violence. Professional thieves over the years have grown more ruthless as armed holdups in Montreal and some U.S. galleries, as well as raids in Paris, have proven. In fact, security guards, vaults and detection equipment seem to challenge the art thief.

Art thieves have a vast and ever-growing territory, unlimited cultural treasures to steal, and an expanding underground network to help them dispose of their loot. As more individuals and institutions place their wealth in art, thefts increase. Additionally, as museums proliferate throughout the United States and Europe, this decreases the amount of artwork available to the private collector. It is a simple case of supply and demand.

Also remember when writing about art theft that the art market has always been international; art crime is now also becoming so. This lends some colorful characters of thieves, fences and purchasers for your novels. Should you be writing about an art theft, it can encompass the globe. The unique quality of the work makes the disposal of artwork the key to profitable criminal activity. Whereas diamonds, gold and other items can be re-cut, melted down or otherwise disguised without too much effect on their resale value, a painting or sculpture is unique. It cannot be altered and retain its original value.

Unlike narcotics, which have to be traded in an illegal market, art has a legitimate market. The thief therefore has to find a means of disposing of his cache and of recirculating it in the legitimate market; once he has achieved this, he is safe, or as safe as he will ever be. The more valuable and well known the target, the greater the degree of risk and the more resourceful his plan of disposal must be. Smuggling objects to another country is one solution because this lessens or postpones the risk of the object's discovery and subsequent identification.

No amount of security or vigilance can stop art thieves as long as prices soar, and masterpieces fetch fabulous sums of money. Even the most efficient art squad lags one step behind determined thieves. It seems that the people who are immersed in the collection of art, antiques and jewelry have themselves forced the price up and are paying for art theft. As for Mauro and me, we're keeping a closer watch on our collection of velvet Elvises!

THREE

Carjacking, Hijacking, Skyjacking and Auto Theft

In the United States, a vehicle is stolen every twenty seconds. Auto theft is an $8 billion a year industry for criminals. Despite the new and ever-increasing security protections designed to foil theft attempts, auto theft is increasing yearly. State lawmakers and the federal government have increased the penalties for automobile thefts because of these statistics.

Surprisingly enough, carelessness in securing vehicles accounts for more than 20 percent of auto theft: one or more of the doors left unlocked, a window left down or partially open, a security system left unactivated. One or more of these items will attract thieves so that when we come out of the store or leave work for the trip home, we find only an empty parking space.

This chapter explores the methods vehicle thieves employ to secure their bounty. It will also explain the various enterprises that today's criminals use to commit their crimes.

Who's the Victim?

Today, vehicle theft is viewed as a victimless crime. The only ones who seem to get hurt are the insurance companies, who increase their fees to offset any losses. If you look at what happens when a vehicle is stolen, one could very easily see the positive side.

Your car is stolen, but you have insurance to cover your loss; therefore, you basically get a new car out of it. The car dealer is happy because you have to buy a new car from him, the car manufacturer is happy because that's one less car in his inventory, the car thief is happy because he's going to make money from stealing the car. If the car is sent to a *chop shop*, they are happy because they can sell the parts from your stolen car to a body repair station for half the price of that of the manufacturer. Now, the body shop is happy because later he can rip off the insurance company by charging full price for the parts he obtained cheaply from the chop shop. The owner of the vehicle that is getting repaired is happy because the body shop owner is absorbing his deductible. So, everybody is happy, and we have a victimless crime.

The only problem with this so-called victimless crime is that we are paying for it in injury, death and property damage caused by criminals fleeing capture. We also pay in the form of higher insurance premiums—some experts believe that a *low* estimation would be between ten and twenty percent; one source stated that twenty-one cents of every dollar in premiums goes to cover fraud and theft losses.

Basic Auto Theft

Juveniles, as young as ten years old, make up the majority of perpetrators who steal automobiles from the streets and parking lots of America. These juvenile offenders know that if apprehended, they will get little or no jail time for their crimes. The going price for a stolen vehicle is around five hundred dollars, so it is easy to see why stealing cars is so attractive to inner-city kids.

Juvenile auto thieves scour streets and parking lots trying to find an unsecured vehicle. By unsecured we mean doors unlocked, windows partly or fully open, and keys in the ignition. If, by chance, the vehicle is unlocked and the keys left inside, which is a petty crime in many localities, our young criminals will get into the vehicle, start it, and drive away to a prearranged location.

Sometimes a chop shop will place an order for a particular type of vehicle. The auto thief will conduct a surveillance of malls, health clubs or upscale lounges and restaurants. One method of this surveillance is to have a passenger van shuttle around a group of car thieves through the aforementioned areas. When a vehicle is located, the driver will stop the van letting out one of his passengers with instructions to steal the vehicle.

The Jimmie

The first option to gain entry into a locked car is to pick the lock. A device called a *jimmie* is used. A jimmie is made from spring steel and is inserted between the window and the rubber trim that protects the inside of the door. The jimmie has a soft rubber or plastic handle on one end and, on the other, a series of notches that can manipulate the lock mechanism. A jimmie can't be used on vehicles where the locking mechanism is electronic.

There are other types of jimmies designed to enter between the rubber window molding and the glass itself. The working end of this jimmie is hooked to the door lock inside the vehicle and just pulled up. Anti-theft door locks are tapered to prevent using a jimmie, but thieves place a piece of tape onto the working end of the jimmie to cause enough friction to pop open the door lock.

Other jimmies are designed to defeat locks located on the side of the door nearer to the dashboard. These jimmies are placed in the same way as above, but closer to the dashboard. For cheap thieves, a simple coat hanger can be bent and twisted into the same configurations as professional jimmies but are less conspicuous if the thief is stopped and questioned by the police.

Ninja Rocks

A new method of gaining entry into vehicles is the *Ninja Rock*—a ⅜-inch cube-shaped white piece of porcelain. It was first used by Southeast Asian gangs. The Ninja Rock, when thrown at a moderate speed, will break and shatter any glass with little or no sound, and can easily be left at a scene with little chance of detection and, therefore, little chance of discovery.

Digital Door Locks

Vehicles with digital or punch-the-numbers door locks are the easiest to gain entry. Just think: You just paid eighteen hundred dollars for this luxury option, and all a car thief has to do to open your door is simply disconnect the battery. Because of an inherent safety feature designed to unlock your doors in case of an accident, your vehicle can easily be opened if it has this type of lock. Our clever young thieves will perform their task and drive away with your car in twenty to thirty seconds.

Computer-Aided Locks

Sophisticated car thieves who go after the more desirable luxury vehicles use a different approach. They will attempt to obtain a key for the vehicle to defeat both the alarm system and locks. The manufacturers of the more expensive luxury vehicles are taking a number of precautions to assure the consumer that their vehicles are protected from theft. Companies have manufactured keys with security devices such as computer chips embedded right on the keys themselves. These vehicles need to be stolen without any damage to them, so the key is mandatory. On most new cars, one key will operate both door locks, the ignition, the glove box and the trunk.

One of the ways to get the key is by obtaining the ignition key code number, which is sometimes found behind the ashtray. The ignition key code number is printed on a sticker inside the door or on the nonvisible inside door lock itself. The key can be duplicated right at the scene by using a portable key maker.

A vehicle can be stolen from a parking garage by either stealing the keys from the attendant's booth, bribing the attendant, or forcing the attendant to turn over the keys of the vehicle marked for theft. In parking garages, if the parking attendant is robbed of the keys, any number of vehicles can be stolen.

Bump and Run

Another method of stealing a luxury car is the *bump and run*. This seems to be the method of choice for obtaining luxury or in-demand vehicles. A bump and run occurs as follows: A chase vehicle follows a luxury car with only the driver in it until a semi-secluded area is available. When the target car is moving slowly, or is stopped, the chase vehicle will then bump into the rear of the vehicle. When the driver jumps out to survey the damage, a second person jumps into the vehicle and drives away. The stolen car is then parked at a nearby parking garage. Once in the garage, the vehicle check-in ticket, used to retrieve the car from the garage, can be sold, or the stolen vehicle can have its license plates changed to avoid detection. It is not uncommon to have this vehicle moved from parking garage to parking garage daily or weekly.

Desirable vehicles are becoming harder and harder to obtain, so thieves have to invent more ways of obtaining these vehicles with little or no damage. Because of these vehicles' protection systems, owners are driving around confident that their vehicle will not be stolen. This confidence tends to aid the thief in his task.

Getting It Started

Once inside the vehicle, there are a number of ways to get it started. If the vehicle is a General Motors or Jeep product, the thief breaks open the left side of the steering column, and inserts a screwdriver directly below the turn signal into a round cup mechanism. This will start the vehicle. To disengage the steering wheel lock, thieves use a device, also used by auto body repairmen and called a *dent puller*, or *slap-hammer*. A dent puller has a plastic or rubber handle on one end and a strong steel self-tapping screw on the other. In the middle is a weighted grip that slides from one end of the tool to the other. Once the screw is inserted into the ignition key slot, the weighted grip is moved back and forth causing the ignition lock to pop out, releasing the steering wheel lock.

If the vehicle is a Ford truck, another system can be used to start the vehicle. Reach under the steering column, pull the ignition wires out, and attach them to the extra ignition locking system, turn the key, and you're off.

Carjacking

The latest trend in stealing cars is carjacking, which is one of the simplest and most straightforward types of crime that exists in America today. Carjacking differs from auto theft in that the vehicle is stolen while the owner is in it as opposed to stealing it without the owner's knowledge. Carjacking generally occurs in urban and densely populated areas as opposed to suburban and rural areas, because once taken by criminals the vehicle can easily be lost in traffic and congestion.

There are many reasons why a vehicle is carjacked:

1. The need for immediate transportation such as after a burglary, armed robbery, murder or kidnapping.
2. To sell the vehicle and use the money for other criminal purposes.
3. Thrillseekers who desire a vehicle to joyride in and who will ultimately abandon the vehicle, sometimes setting it on fire. This is most frequently done by teenagers. Sometimes gangs in urban ghettos require this as an initiation into the gang.
4. The carjacker intends to kidnap the person operating the vehicle and will use the car to take the owner to an area where the owner will be raped, murdered,

robbed, beaten or abandoned.

The frequency of carjacking has created a market for alarms to combat it: self-defense weapons, ranging from mini-stun guns to mace, hot pepper spray, and electronic alarms that scream with ninety decibels or more of pulsating power. Carjacking is a direct physical confrontation, which could either go smoothly, the operator simply gives up his car, or more dangerously, there is a struggle and the operator ends up injured or killed.

Because carjacking occurs at such a fast pace—the owner is immediately demanded to exit the vehicle or drive the carjacker somewhere—it is the type of crime that is fraught with tremendous stress. Carjackers should be portrayed in your works as highly stressed individuals willing to take tremendous risks and willing to carry out threats.

Because of the violence associated with carjackings, Congress passed the Anti-Car Theft Act of 1992, which makes carjacking a federal offense. If apprehended and convicted of carjacking, the penalties imposed are much more severe than for regular car theft, so severe that not only are carjackers heavily fined, they can be sentenced to life in prison.

Methods of Carjacking

Here are few ways carjackers operate:

Carjacking at a Mall Parking Lot. This is one of the most popular and easiest carjackings to perform. The carjacker waits between cars or leans against a car and waits for the person to enter their vehicle. A carjacker will usually wait by vehicles parked far away from the stores so that there are not many people around to witness the incident. Some people park far away, because they have brand new vehicles and do not want them dented by other car doors opening against them.

Once the person puts the key in the door lock and unlocks the car, the carjacker has access to the vehicle, the person and the keys. During 1992 and 1993, Mauro and I experienced in our law enforcement area a tremendous surge in these types of carjackings, especially around Christmas. Although many people thought the carjackers intended to steal the vehicle and rob them, it appeared many of these carjackers ultimately took their female victims hostage, robbed them *and* raped them.

Sometimes, carjackers will actually find a car whose owner has left it open and hide in the backseat waiting for the owner to return. In this scenario the owner knows the door is open and will simply enter the car and place the key in the ignition. Then he or she is suddenly confronted by a knife- or gun-wielding carjacker. At this point the carjacker will order the person to either exit the vehicle and leave his keys or to drive him to a location where the person is robbed, raped or sometimes murdered.

Another method is to have a different carjacker pretend to examine a tire or will make a tire flat. The "disabled car" is next to the target vehicle. When the victim returns to her car, the carjacker will strike up a conversation about his "dilemma" in having his tires go flat on him, even though the vehicle may not belong to the carjacker. He may then ask the woman to contact the police for him or to give him a lift to the nearest service station so that he can get assistance. Of course, once inside the woman's vehicle, he begins his reign of terror.

We have seen many instances in recent years where carjackers have forced the owner of a car from their vehicle in a mall parking lot and taken off only to find that they have an infant in the backseat. We have never heard of an incident in which the infant was harmed; usually the vehicle is abandoned a short time later. It seems as if infants are too much for carjackers to handle.

Random Carjacking in Urban Areas. This type of carjacking occurs when a vehicle has pulled up to either a stop sign or a red light in a largely urban and heavily populated area. The carjacker walks up to the driver's window, produces a handgun or a knife, menaces the person with it, and orders the owner either to step out or to move over, at which point the carjacker will jump into the vehicle.

When Joe was working as a detective for the Brooklyn District Attorney's Office, he investigated an incident that could only happen in New York. A woman was driving her car on Flatbush Avenue near Long Island College when she was carjacked at a red light. The carjacker approached her vehicle on foot from behind, pulled open the door, and produced a handgun. He shoved the handgun in the woman's face and ordered her to step out of the car. The woman, terrified, was thrown to the ground and the carjacker sped off in her vehicle, south on Flatbush Avenue.

The carjacker headed to the East New York section of Brooklyn. While the carjacker was stopped at a stop sign on the corner of Herzl Street, he had his carjacked vehicle carjacked! Yes, that's right, while carjacker #1 was stopped, another carjacker appeared, opened the door of the vehicle, and attempted to pull carjacker #1 out. Carjacker #2, realizing that the occupant was armed, produced a handgun and a gun battle ensued right in the street.

Carjacker #2 was mortally wounded; however, carjacker #1 was shot in the neck and still lying on the ground when the police arrived. The police, thinking that carjacker #1 was the owner of the vehicle, and, therefore, the victim, removed him to the hospital where he was treated and interviewed. Carjacker #1, smart enough to realize that no one knew he had carjacked the vehicle, pretended to be the owner. Of course, once his identity was confirmed and the report of the original carjacking in another section of Brooklyn filtered down, carjacker #1 was arrested by detectives.

On other occasions the carjacker will attempt entry from the passenger side. He produces a knife or gun and orders the driver to take him to a particular location or to simply drive around until further instructions are given. This type of carjacker has an emergency and selects the vehicle simply by which one is most convenient.

The only way to avoid being carjacked in these circumstances is to lock your doors and keep your windows rolled up so a carjacker cannot easily obtain entry into a vehicle.

Suburbs and Rural Areas. A carjacker will usually walk in front of a vehicle that has come to a stop or is at a light and pretend to pass out. At this point ninety-nine percent of drivers will exit the vehicle to see if the person is all right. The carjacker produces a knife or a handgun and commandeers the car.

The Bump and Take. A person will be operating their car on a road when they will suddenly be tapped from behind by another vehicle. While the victim and the carjacker exit their vehicles to check the damage, a passenger from the carjacker's vehicle will come around and steal the car. Quite often the vehicle used to bump the first vehicle was also carjacked, or stolen. This way, carjackers get two cars within a very short period of time.

Chop Shops

Chop shop is a law enforcement slang name for a location where stolen vehicles are dismantled and the parts sold off to garages and body shops at below market value. Most vehicles that are stolen are sold to chop shop operations for around five hundred dollars. These chop shops strip the vehicle and can make an enormous cash return on their investment, as much as double the initial selling price of the vehicle.

Chop shops can be found just about anywhere—even in the street, mostly the dead-end type. Vacant lots on dead-end streets are ideal because the trees located on these lots can be used to lift an engine or transmission out of the vehicle by using a chain over a strong branch. A car can be stripped of all sellable parts in under half an hour by a group of professionals. By removing twenty bolts, the whole front end, including the hood, both fenders, bumper and grill, can be separated from the vehicle. Front ends on late model cars are most desirable because they are used as replacement parts for vehicles damaged in accidents—and front end damage is the most common result of an accident.

Another profitable section of a stolen vehicle is the rear end for the same reason. On late-model vehicles, replacement parts are hard to find because of the demand for the complete vehicle. These parts are extremely difficult to trace because there are no markings that will indicate they were removed from a particular vehicle.

The newest item to steal from vehicles is the air bag. Air bags are sold legitimately for around $1200; stolen air bags are sold for $200 to $500. The bags are stolen and sold to auto repair shops to be installed in vehicles with accident damage to replace used air bags. Thieves have to be careful when stealing these items as setting them off makes them useless.

Chop shops have one or more of the following indications that illegal activity is being conducted: Juveniles are the leading individuals when it comes to stealing vehicles, so you will see the same faces of young people hanging around these shops. Once the word is out that a location is buying stolen vehicles, our young thieves will attempt to please their buyers by following through with their needs.

Junk yards make ideal locations for chop shops because they are usually out of public sight, making it difficult to observe everyday operations. These yards often get their vehicles from owners who are dissatisfied with their present vehicle because of expensive car payments, mechanical problems, high mileage, or they just don't want the vehicle anymore. The owner of the vehicle pays a small fee and his vehicle is dismantled by the junk yard. All parts that have the vehicle identification number (often referred to as the VIN) will be destroyed by crushing. The owner will then report the vehicle stolen and collect his insurance.

Chop shops are also used to make stolen vehicles legal. Skilled personnel can alter the vehicle identification numbers. This craftsman can earn as much as $3,500 per vehicle. Vehicle identification number plates are carefully removed from vehicles totalled in accidents and then installed onto the stolen vehicles. The stolen vehicle can then be registered. Chop shops also use counterfeit credentials to obtain valid titles.

Chop shops also make a profit from odometer rollback. An odometer rollback is performed to reduce high mileage on a vehicle that is fairly new to increase its market value or comply with a lease agreement. The National Highway Traffic Safety Association reported that odometer rollback annual loss is between $3 and $4 billion. One way to roll back the odometer is to falsify the title prior to resale. Another method is to first detail the vehicle to improve the way it looks: a good wash and waxing, new tires, floor carpeting, brake and gas pedals. A person known in the trade as a *clocker* physically turns back the odometer, which only takes a few minutes using screwdrivers and lock picks. These vehicles can then be sold at auction houses or to used car dealers for an increased profit.

Many chop shops are located in small garages in a residential community. These garages will be detached from the main house and out of view of the street. Inside these garages will be the tools necessary to completely strip the vehicles using a minimal amount of time. There will be an engine hoist, assorted jacks, air compressor, power and hand tools. To avoid detection, one vehicle will be disassembled at a time. The only problem with operations like this is the disposal of unsellable portions. The metal portions can be torched, that is cut up using a welding torch, or cut using various hand and motorized metal saws. These parts can be transported to a salvage yard and sold as scrap.

The other nonsellable pieces, cloths and other material that are worthless, can be disposed of as trash. The only problem with this is that apprehension is likely if an endless supply of nonuseable automobile parts is found in the trash. Some of our backyard chop shops will make midnight raids to unauthorized dumping locations to dispose of their unmarketable goods.

Because chop shops want to avoid detection, they will transport their items for sale in unmarked pickups, light hauling vans or trucks. This is a red flag to the police be-

Vehicle Identification Numbers (VIN)

For those of you who don't quite understand the importance of VINs, we will take a moment to explain it. Go out to your vehicle and look into your car through the windshield to the top of your dashboard on the driver's side. Sometimes it will be on the windshield post on the driver's side. The VIN is on a small rectangular plate attached to the car with two rivets, one on each side. These rivets are unique in themselves because their heads, the part which is visible to you, have a shape for each make of vehicle. We are told that these rivets are a controlled item and cannot be purchased readily. The VIN itself is seventeen characters, both letters and numbers. This series of characters specifies the vehicle's make, model, type, and where and when it was manufactured. The VIN is also stamped on the engine and transmission and may sometimes be found on a sticker on the driver's side door. Each manufacturer also places the VIN in a hidden location somewhere on the frame, as a last resort to identify the vehicle if the engine or transmission is missing or has been replaced. The manufacturer changes the location of the "hidden VIN" each year. Only the manufacturer, insurance companies and law enforcement agencies know the location of the hidden VIN.

When a police officer is comparing the VINs on the vehicle's registration and the VIN plate behind the windshield, he may also check the sticker on the door. If this sticker is missing, this is a good indicator to the police officer that something is wrong.

---

cause legitimate businesses advertise on the side of their vehicles.

Buildings used for chop shops can be legitimate automobile repair or collision repair centers. To avoid detection, off hour late nights and weekends are used to cut up illegally obtained vehicles. These legitimate establishments will increase their business by installing stolen vehicle parts onto accident-damaged vehicles at a cheaper rate. One good indicator that a legitimate dealer is using stolen vehicle parts is absorbing a large insurance deductible in the repair cost of the damaged vehicle.

Vehicles Stolen for Export

Stolen vehicles for export into Central and South America, the Caribbean and Mexico are in high demand. Mexico is mainly used as a location for chop shops because of a treaty which states that stolen vehicles must be returned to the United States. Mexico is the only country that has this treaty stipulation. Because of the number of mountainous regions and poor road conditions in Central America, South America and the Caribbean, the preferred vehicles are 4 × 4-wheel drives. Officials will make no attempt in these countries to put a halt to the import of these vehicles. A good portion of these stolen vehicles are used by government agencies and upper-class residents. Because of this, the cars must be undamaged and are stolen with the keys.

Once the vehicles are stolen, they are shipped out of the country through freight haulers—commercial shipping lines that use steel shipping containers, which can contain up to two vehicles. To get through United States Customs Service, they use forged documents with altered VINs or inaccurate shipping contents (the vehicles are usually listed as household goods).

In the Caribbean, a law enforcement study reported that one out of every five vehicles shipped from the United States showed signs of being stolen. For vehicles valued over $16,000, the percentage changed to four of every five vehicles stolen from the United States. The amazing thing to remember is that there is a waiting list of buyers who will pay as much as twice the original purchase price of the vehicle knowing it was stolen from the United States. Luxury and 4 × 4-wheel drive vehicles are very hard to come by in developing countries. Wealthy customers are willing to pay the extra price for these vehicles, creating a high demand for stolen cars.

An important consideration in exporting stolen vehicles is the distance the vehicle must be moved to reach a port. Car thieves do not want to get caught and this can easily occur when transporting the stolen vehicle to the port. One method to avoid apprehension is to haul the stolen vehicles in a car carrier. Car carriers, unless they violate a traffic law, are unlikely to be stopped. One problem with this method of transportation is that legitimate car carriers transport one make of vehicle. When transporting stolen vehicles, multiple makes are on board—a red flag for law enforcement.

The United States Customs Service, in an attempt to slow the shipping of stolen vehicles out of the country, applies for and receives regulations that place a time limit on vehicles for export. The vehicles must be registered several days before shipping—enough time that the proper inspection and credential-checking can be performed. Unfortunately, resourceful thieves can circumvent this. They purchase a vehicle from an automobile dealership and ship it to a country. Then they remove the VIN plates, the paperwork, and the plates, send them back to the United States and place them on a similar, but stolen, vehicle. This stolen vehicle is then shipped following regular procedures from the United States to the country where it was requested.

Gray Market Vehicles

A gray market vehicle is basically any vehicle manufactured in a foreign country for use in that country and not for export into the United States. These vehicles are not made according to the United States's emissions and safety standards and often have defects that could result in fires and poor performance; some even lack rearview and passenger-side mirrors. These vehicles are usually represented as vehicles that have been converted to United States standards, but nothing has been changed.

Gray market vehicles are ideal candidates for insurance fraud because they are cheaper to obtain, thus making market value higher than purchase price. The owner can purchase the gray market vehicle, sell it to a chop shop, report it stolen, and recoup a sizable profit from the insurance company.

Heavy Industrial and Construction Equipment

Insurance companies estimate that heavy industrial construction and farm vehicle thefts create a billion dollar a year loss. These types of vehicles contain few if any antitheft devices and some can even be started without a key. They are easy targets because they are often found in vacant lots and in rural areas. The method our thieves use is very simple: They climb aboard, start the engine, and drive away. Sometimes the vehicles are placed onto a semi-tractor trailer. This operation requires at least two people.

Once the vehicle is obtained, it will be sold using phony documentation, either by direct sale or auction. There is little or no paperwork involved with these vehicles because they are not registered since they are mostly driven off-road. The only identification on some of these vehicles is an engine number, so fraudulent paperwork is easy to obtain.

Hijacking

Remember that the hijacking of today is an interesting renewal of the hijacking that occurred in the ancient history of this country. Stagecoaches, trucks, caravans, merchant ships and other types of transportation have, in their time, been taken by what was known in the past as "highlanding." But, the modern hijacker has exceeded his predecessors in both the amount of earnings and in the finesse and skill required.

In a single hijacking, several hundred thousand dollars worth of easily marketable merchandise is available. This is because the capacity of the modern tractor trailer truck is enormous. The items taken during a hijacking are usually consumer-oriented goods, which can easily be sold. Items such as liquor, television sets, refrigerators, washing machines, and cigarettes are commonly stolen.

Truck hijacking seems to be mainly an organized crime caper. We all know that teamsters have a certain amount of organized crime behind them. Because of this, schedules, routes, drivers and cargo can all be manipulated for the benefit of the thieves.

Hijacking while the vehicle is in motion on its route takes a series of operations that require skillful planning, perfect timing and expert execution. At the peak level of organization, a hijacking gang will work in the following manner: The *fingerman* (usually an employee of a trucking firm) informs the gang of an expected shipment, including the nature of the merchandise, the schedule, the make of the truck, and the license plate number. The *spotter* points out the truck to the men actually doing the hijacking and follows it to the *drop* (area where merchandise is unloaded). The gunmen stop the truck at a prearranged location and either remove the driver to their car or bind, gag and place him in the hijacked truck.

A hijacker without a reliable fence is at a very serious disadvantage. The fence plays a major role in the success of these types of crimes. Many hijackings are steal-to-order jobs. Once a truck is targeted and selected because of the cargo it carries, organized crime will investigate the vulnerability of the trucking company for a theft. Many times the hijacked loads are sold to persons even before they are stolen. You may recall during the gasoline shortage of the 1970s a rash of gasoline truck hijackings.

The Shipping Process

Let's talk about the shipping process, which hijackers are very familiar with. About 50 percent of all hijackings are inside jobs. Let's follow a carton of clothing being shipped from Harry's Hotpants in New York City to Mimi's Minis in Miami, Florida:

The Packager. At Harry's Hotpants (the shipper), the goods are carefully packed in cardboard containers, which are then steel strapped. The name and address of Mimi's is placed on labels stuck to the side of each carton. The order numbers are also placed on the side of each box.

The Traffic Manager. He prepares what is known as a bill of lading in triplicate describing the shipment and giving it an order number.

The Shipping Clerk. The shipping clerk of Harry's calls the trucking company to request that they make a pick-up.

The Dispatcher. After receiving the request from the shipping clerk, the dispatcher of the trucking company orders one of the drivers working in the neighborhood to make the pick-up.

The City Pick-Up Driver. The driver makes the pick-up after first checking the packaging and the labeling of each carton. He proceeds to the motor freight terminal. Best practices require him to close and lock a steel folding gate after each pick-up.

The Freight Terminal Action. At the motorfreight terminal, the shipment is unloaded onto a platform by the truck driver who picked it up. A manifest is written and the traffic and billing department of the transportation company receives the bill of lading. A waybill number is assigned to the shipment.

Terminal Loading. The shipment is then placed on a trailer, the doors are closed, and the transportation company lock is affixed together with the numbered, impressed seal. The seal number is recorded by the dispatcher. The seal number is also placed on the manifest and on the road driver's dispatch order. This is a separate seal number used just to protect the integrity of the shipment.

Alarm System. The trailer is then assigned to a tractor. Ideally, it is equipped with an automatic alarm that will sound a warning if it is disturbed at any time while in transit or unattended. The alarm is set by the dispatcher at the terminal with a master key. Some of the alarms, which you may have seen on the sides of trucks, are manufactured by Babaco. This alarm can now be turned off only by the dispatcher in Miami, Florida, with his master key.

The Road Drivers. The driver receives his instructions

from the dispatcher: he is to be relieved by two other drivers in relay along the Eastern Seaboard route. In compliance with Inter-State Commerce Commission regulations, he will maintain a driver's log showing the times of driving and the times of rest. As an additional check, some tractors are equipped with an instrument that records automatically the periods of driving and stopping as well as the speed of the vehicle.

Arrival. Upon reaching the Miami terminal, the driver checks in with the Miami dispatcher and gives him a report of the trip, a copy of the logs, and a pouch containing bills and instructions concerning the load. The shipment is then unloaded and checked against the manifest. It is imperative, at this point, that the seal has not been disturbed. If that seal is broken, of course, it will mean that someone has had access to the shipment while it was in transit from Harry's Hotpants to Mimi's Minis.

The City Delivery. At the Miami terminal, the cartons are checked and loaded into a city or local delivery truck, which goes to Mimi's clothing warehouse. The doors are unlocked and the cartons are placed on the platform where they are checked by the receiving clerk who signs the waybill. He may mark the cartons with the date and time of delivery and a symbol to indicate if they were in acceptable condition.

Let's say our bad guy reviews the shipping orders and knows that a truckload of brand new, top-of-the-line, large-screen TVs is being transported from San Francisco to New York City. Using their influence, the bad guys install a driver loyal to the cause. This driver will be given a route to follow, but prior to arriving in New York City, a slight detour will occur. In some out of the way place, the driver, along with his accomplices, will either unload the cargo into a waiting tractor trailer, or give up the tractor trailer itself. To make it appear realistic, the driver may even be tied up or assaulted. The driver will then continue on his merry way avoiding any law enforcement inspection stops or weight stations. Once the driver feels his accomplices are safe and secure, he will contact the local law enforcement agency and report the crime.

The same scheme could be used on shorter runs. We have both worked on numerous cases where, of all things, seafood trucks have been hijacked. New Jersey has a substantial number of seafood restaurants, co-ops and fish markets. Seafood is very expensive and practically nontraceable. We all know a fish is a fish and has no vehicle registration numbers, so tracing these edible delights is impossible. Just about all the seafood-truck hijackings we have worked on, even though it wasn't always proven, seemed to have had an insider. When we talk about seafood trucks, we're talking about medium-sized, refrigerated panel trucks.

Less than semi-size trucks are usually hijacked at truck stops. A gunman will direct the driver to a semi-secluded area where the transfer is made. Waiting in this area is a truck similar in size to the hijacked one. A number of accomplices will be standing by and, in just about all the ones we have worked on, these accomplices will be wearing some type of ski mask or other face covering to prevent recognition. All will be wearing gloves, not only to not leave any fingerprints, but to aid in carrying the heavy crates. Once the transfer is made, the driver of the hijacked vehicle will be made to walk back to the road or be tied up and left to be discovered. The only problem with tying the driver is the criminals must make certain that the victim will be discovered quickly before the victim is injured or dies from exposure to the elements.

Trucks containing merchandise are sometimes parked on city streets or in fenced-in parking lots. These trucks usually have just a padlock, which can easily be cut with a pair of bolt cutters. Local street gangs find this easy prey; they either climb over or cut through the fence, go to either the rear or side door and cut the padlock to gain entry. Once inside, a quick survey will be conducted, and items are removed. They seldom take all the cargo, usually just what they can carry.

Another technique for truck hijacking occurs when a

trucker pulls into a truck stop for some food and fuel. While at the truck stop, the truck driver will meet a very friendly lady who will persuade him to give her a ride down the road. Once on their way, the lady brandishes a weapon and forces the driver to a location where her accomplices are waiting to receive the merchandise.

How Police Capture Hijackers

There are common methods the police use to link hijackers to the crime:

1. Sideview mirrors, rearview mirrors, window, cab door ledges and handles, side and rear doors, are the most likely places where hijackers leave fingerprints. This is one of the reasons that some hijackers wear gloves. Another reason is to avoid drawing attention to themselves, as many truck drivers wear leather gloves.
2. Any dirt left inside the truck cab such as soil on the clutch peddle can be linked to shoes, which may be found later by the police. As you know, dirt and soil from a particular area can be positively linked to the same type of soil when it is discovered inside the treads of the criminal's shoes.
3. Anything that may be partially on the hijacker and partially left in the cab, such as matchbooks, will not be left behind by the professional hijacker.
4. Shoe and heel prints. Of course some hijackers may be aware that cartons found in the body of the truck will have to be stepped on and climbed over. Additionally, in the haste of unloading and ripping open cartons to reveal merchandise and reload it, many times heel and shoe prints will be left on cartons. The experienced hijacker will destroy these cartons at a different site or burn the trailer with the cartons on site after the load is transferred.
5. The distance traveled. By estimating the distance in which the truck has traveled, clues can be obtained by detectives in regard to the neighborhood of the drop. The odometer reading can be taken and compared to

the mileage recorded when the tank was last filled with gas. The amount of gasoline in the truck is a good indication of the upper limit of the radius of the operation. Some experienced hijackers have been known to drain the tank completely of gasoline, which is very easy to do simply by using a hose as a syphon. Sometimes hijackers will disembowel the internal components of an odometer to make the actual mileage traveled impossible to detect.

6. The top of the cab. The New York City Safe, Loft and Truck Squad initiated an operational procedure many years ago to paint the top of the cab with numbers. In case the truck was hijacked it could be easily observed by helicopters. Of course the top of the cab is usually huge and the numbers are painted as large as possible. When we are dealing with hijackings that are well-planned and well-organized, the fingerman will have all of the information of the truck, so the hijackers come prepared with paint to match the top of the cab.
7. Informants. Criminals know as well as the police that warehouse employees, former criminals, gas station attendants, and self-service or road service people are frequently interviewed to determine if they can ascertain the location and descriptions of people that participated in the hijacking.

Skyjacking

Skyjacking is the most dramatic and highly visible form of terrorism even though it is not the most frequently employed. Skyjacking illustrates perfectly all of the elements of terrorist crimes and so is perhaps the most useful of examples. It is also the form of terrorism that presents the most personal risk to American citizens.

Approximately thirty years have passed since skyjacking became a familiar word to the American public. Today the crime remains the same but the stakes are far higher, for skyjacking is a weapon of terror turned against America.

It threatens not only those who might find themselves on a hostage plane, but all of us who are concerned with the future of our nation.

The Sky Marshal Program was proposed by President Nixon in October 1970 and was one part of the United States government's response to the threat of skyjacking in general and to Palestinian skyjackings in particular. The other part of this deterrence program was the widespread installation of metal detectors in airports and the introduction of passenger and baggage searches. Congress appropriated the funds and the airlines budgeted hundreds of thousands of dollars to support the program.

You wouldn't exactly call the Sky Marshals' job an enviable one. Presumably the attractions of the job include travel to exotic and faraway places, independent work free from supervision, and carrying a gun legally. The dangers of the job outweigh these benefits, however.

Today's skyjacker does not fit into any one mold or physical description. Skyjacking is a violent means of getting a free ride and gratifying a need at the expense of other people. Of course the skyjacker is seldom a thief, however, he may be a malcontent, a dropout from everyday life, a political fanatic, a rebel with or without a cause, or an emotional disaster; he may be literate or illiterate, college-educated or have just barely finished the third grade. He may have long hair or a crewcut. He may wear expensive suits or cheap ones. He may be a cool, intellectual professional or a whimpering coward. Either way, there is no single pattern to skyjackings or skyjackers.

Some skyjack cases bear close relationships to others while others are unique. In the United States, the Federal Aviation Administration, which regulates the airlines, have psychologists who have been trying to develop a profile of skyjackers for years. It is they who first conducted interviews with what we might call "deactivated" skyjackers—those who failed or who returned home after discovering that there was no haven for them at the end of the line. They also interviewed families of skyjackers who did not return. It was on the basis of this extensive research that the behavioral profile of a skyjacker was devised. However, this profile has been critized for a number of reasons, among them that it is too broad and based only on American skyjackers and does not have universal applications.

Why Skyjack?

Why of all things would you want to grab an airplane? Psychologists have offered different reasons about symbolism and flight and the power of commandeering but to us there is one basic reason: Because the plane happens to be there. Skyjacking is one of the current forms of protest. It is our opinion that skyjackers fall into five, sometimes overlapping, categories: criminals on the run; individuals with personal or political reasons; people or groups with organized political motivations; emotional disaster cases; losers and misfits.

Now, based on these groupings let's take a closer look at the types of skyjackers and how they operate.

Categories of Skyjackers

It has been said that skyjacking has evolved during the last fifty years into the following divisions:

1. Escaping refugees, 1947-1952, 1958-1972, 1980s
2. Transportation, 1961-1994
3. The mentally unbalanced, 1961-1994
4. Political terrorists, 1968-1988
5. Escaping criminals, 1971-1973
6. Extortion, 1971-1973, 1975-1977
7. Religious fundamentalists, 1983-1988
8. Bomb saboteurs, 1984-1994

Escaping Refugees. The escaping refugee skyjacker will seize an aircraft to flee from an oppressive political regime. Under international law, certain immunities or exemptions for foreign aircraft and its occupants entering in distress are recognized. In a majority of these cases, a degree of immunity has been granted to aircraft including those arriving under the control of skyjackers. Political asylum has been given to skyjackers trying to escape from countries whose governments deny or disregard human rights and who do not permit their citizens to leave the country lawfully. This type of skyjacker is usually a desperate and ruthless person and will stop at nothing to get to freedom.

Transportation. Unlike political refugees, this type of skyjacker uses the aircraft simply as a convenient means of traveling without cost or the legal formalities of entering and departing countries. The majority of these cases involve Castro's supporters in Colombia, Venezuela, and the United States, since no regularly scheduled commercial air service operates between these counties, and Cuba is one of the easiest countries to divert an aircraft to unlawfully. This category also includes persons who cannot afford the airfare so they skyjack the plane! This type of skyjacker flew mostly between 1961-1972, but is still a possibility, especially in today's tough economy.

The Mentally Unbalanced Person. This type of skyjacker will use any method to attract attention. They can prove that they can be an effective human being by commandeering airplanes, or so they believe. The skyjacker also feels that he can start anew by gaining fame and glory. In short, this type of person is plagued by mental, emotional and social problems and seeks wide publicity to offset personal failures in life.

Political Terrorists. These criminals skyjack planes or sabotage them in the air, but they have also attacked airports and used any form of disruption or hostage-taking that would enable them to put the pressure on governments. This type of air piracy for protest is often used for political blackmail. Perhaps the most widely known are the actions of the Palestinian Front for the Liberation of Palestine, but other groups have skyjacked including the Black Panthers, the Japanese Red Army, the Croatians, the Armenians and Sikhs. This type of skyjacker will usually use either implied or actual bombs to threaten those on board the plane.

Escaping Criminals. These persons and others with criminal backgrounds use skyjacking to escape trial or prosecution. Also included in this group are criminals being transported from one area to another within the United States who hope to escape and avoid their current sentences.

Extortion. In recent years, skyjacking attempts for profit have become common. On numerous occasions they have included the robbery of individual passengers as well as ransom demands to insure the safety of the airplane passengers and crew. They can be categorized as Jesse James skyjackings. In 1972 there was one seventeen-week period in which there was a skyjacking every single Friday. The last day of the work week became known as "Skyjack Friday." It took a great deal of effort and severe prison sentences to bring this category of skyjacking under control. This type of skyjacker is not considered to be as dangerous or as deadly.

Religious Fundamentalists. In 1982, skyjacking of aircraft by Islamic Fundamentalists began. During the next two years, seven skyjackings were engineered by the Shiite Muslims in Lebanon. There were also numerous skyjackings to and from Iran during the civil war between the religious and secular forces of that country. These type of skyjackers are ready to die for their cause and innocent Western passengers are of no particular concern to them. This type of skyjacker is considered one of the most dangerous.

Bomb Saboteurs. Bomb saboteurs are new and deadly to air piracy. The saboteur is a clever technician who plays the role of the hidden brain behind some of the most devastating skyjack schemes and is never found at the scene of the crime. From his concealed headquarters, whether it be his living room or his place of business, the saboteur sends lethal weapons of destruction onto planes full of passengers. Sometimes these deadly instruments are carried by their own people, but more often they are placed in the luggage of a passenger who boards the plane unaware. The advent of plastic explosives and their use against airplanes has caught airplane security by surprise, giving the bomb saboteur an enormous advantage. He is an evil genius who is challenging air security as never before. The most recent type of skyjacking involving this type of criminal was Pan Am Flight 103, which exploded over Lockerbie, Scotland.

Vessels and Aircrafts

Pleasure boats are nice toys that many wish they could have. Sometimes, people purchase them even when they can't afford a boat. Eventually, payments become delinquent and they have to get rid of it. So, what do they do? They can hire someone to steal it, take it to a marina, and send it to a boat chop shop. All usable parts are removed and the rest is either set on fire or sunk.

If the vessel is a fast cigarette boat, drug smugglers may steal the boat to meet a mother ship out at sea, and then, much like bootleggers, bring the cargo back to shore. Because these boats are only used one time, they are usually damaged by hot wiring and then run ashore. Hot wiring is a way of diverting the ignition switch by cutting and connecting the ignition wires, thus, no need for a key. It is not uncommon at the end of the job to torch the boat in an attempt to hide any evidence that may be left behind.

Boats are also stolen for export to other countries. They may be taken from their docks, or more commonly with bigger vessels, they are forcibly boarded while under way at sea. Once aboard, the pirates either kill or put the crew out to sea in emergency life boats.

Aircrafts are stolen either for parts (removed at aircraft chop shops) or to be used to transport narcotics from Central and South America into the United States. An insider at an airport turns over the keys for the aircraft or the aircraft is hijacked. Because of the need for secrecy, the pilots are usually killed.

Because of the Federal RICO statute, the vehicles used in a commission of a crime are forfeited to the government. It is much easier and less costly to steal vehicles, vessels and aircrafts to be used in the transportation of illegal contraband.

F O U R

CON ARTISTS

A con artist's greatest feat is to remove money from your pocket and place it into his without putting a scratch on you or threatening physical violence. It is a saying among police detectives that any punk can grab a gun and rob you, but it takes a special, smart, cunning and sophisticated person to be a good con artist.

Salesmen of Fraud

When you write about con artists, remember one thing: They are very flamboyant characters. They are salesmen whose product is fraud. Being defined as a nonviolent crime, swindling involves elements of intentional deceit, concealment, corruption, and misrepresentation to gain the property of another, and it is facilitated by the willing cooperation of unaware or unknowing victims. Because of this trickery, the victim is often silent. Either the victim does not realize that a fraud has been perpetrated, or he is unwilling to report it for fear of being branded a sucker by his friends or the police. In New York City, the con artist capital of the world, the police department groups this type of crime under "crimes against persons."

Con artists are motivated by one thing: money, money and more money! To truly appreciate a con artist, you must watch him in action. When you take the time to observe a con artist, it is almost a shame to see the energy and intelligence expended in fraud. Since con artists are flamboyant, you might portray them as eccentric, outgoing and overzealous. In the pecking order of criminals, they are slightly above the sediment, because they actually use their intelligence, rather than brute force, to steal.

Take for instance Frank Abagnale, who was one of the most successful con artists in the history of the United States. For five years Mr. Abagnale worked as a pilot with Pan American Airlines and worked himself up through the cockpit from flight engineer to captain, all with a simple Pan Am identification card. Although he was a high school drop out, Abagnale passed the bar exam on his third try, and with a false Harvard Law Transcript practiced law in Baton Rouge, Louisiana. He also became a pediatrics consultant at a hospital in Atlanta, Georgia, after reading only a handful of medical books and producing a false degree from Columbia University in New York City. He was also a Professor of Sociology at Brigham Young University. In all these places Abagnale picked up the jargon of the trade, discovered the perks of each job, and bilked company after company of either cash or free business expenses.

Quick Change/Short Change Artists

These con artists do a flimflam with money, and only need a twenty dollar bill and a one dollar bill to make quick cash, so they are in business very quickly. Often times they only need to go to a young or inexperienced cashier in a store that is so busy the cashier is only more willing to get rid of a difficult customer as soon as possible.

Restaurants are very good marks for these types of con artists. This is a complicated scheme for those of us who don't have natural criminal tendencies, so here's a breakdown of how it works:

1. The con artist enters a restaurant and purchases a small item such as a cup of coffee, so the entire check is less than one dollar. He drinks his coffee, and check in hand, heads for the cashier.
2. He produces a twenty dollar bill for payment to the cashier. As soon as he hands the cashier the money, he begins to talk to the cashier about something that is good enough to interest her: the news of the day, a local event, or something personal such as her hair, lipstick or figure. Remember, con artists are really actors, so he must be debonair—someone a female clerk wouldn't mind taking compliments from.
3. The cashier places the twenty dollar bill in the register while trying to count and pay attention to the customer. She lays the change from the twenty on the counter. The con artist will pick up the small change but not touch the paper money. At the same time he will ask for another item such as a pack of cigarettes.
4. While the cashier reaches for the cigarettes, he removes a one dollar bill from his pocket. As he pays the cashier the exact change for the cigarettes, he holds up the one dollar bill and says to her, "Wow, that's unbelievable, here I had a dollar bill in my pocket all the time and I didn't know it."
5. The con will keep this dollar bill in sight in one hand, while reaching with the same hand for the nineteen dollars change on the counter from his original purchase. But as his hand approaches the money he folds up the one dollar bill with a swift motion and palms it. At the same time, with another single move, he folds up the ten dollar bill in such a way that it is hidden with the remaining nine one dollar bills (or five and four ones).

6. All the time, the con man is asking the cashier another question about something trivial and looking her straight in the eye. He then holds the nineteen dollars in plain sight, with the ten dollar bill secreted within the other nine dollars. The cashier, if she thinks of it at all, thinks that he has placed the single dollar bill he "discovered" in his pocket with the money still in his hand.
7. Since change is always in demand, he asks if she would like to give him a ten dollar bill for the ten ones. He hands her the pile with one hand and takes her ten dollar bill with the other. He promptly pockets the ten dollars and starts for the door.
8. Usually, the con man will pause to light a cigarette, giving the cashier time to discover that she has nineteen dollars instead of ten one dollar bills. He stalls until she tells him of the mistake, or, in the event the cashier overlooks the mistake or decides to pocket the extra nine dollars herself, he returns as though he has suddenly discovered the discrepancy. If the cashier calls him back (and most will), she will show him the nineteen dollars and tell him that he has shortchanged himself. The con man will thank her profusely for her honesty and combine it with the other compliments about her face or figure.
9. But wait, here comes the most important part of the con. The con man will then bring forth the single dollar bill that he had palmed and toss it down with the other nineteen dollars, suggesting once again to the cashier that she may need the change and asking her for a twenty dollar bill in return.

So, for his twenty-one dollars and five minutes, the con artist walks out of the restaurant with thirty-one dollars! Ambitious con artists register as many as twenty or thirty scores a day. Some scores have been known to occur twice in the same place on the same day, because the shortages are very seldom noticed until the count is made at the close of the day's business when the register is counted out.

These swindles are not always done by men; several women have become very efficient working shops where young men handle the cash registers. You guessed it, the womanly sex appeal added to the talk leaves the young cashier boys with nothing but memories.

Another short change scam is the envelope switch, which is very easy. The con artist enters a store and offers a handful of bills and small change for a twenty dollar bill. The cashier, only too happy to get small bills and change, will do it. The con artist takes from her pocket a stamped, addressed envelope and says to the cashier, "This is so I can send the twenty dollar bill to my mother for her birthday." After receiving the twenty dollar bill, and while the clerk is counting the money, she puts the bill in the envelope, seals it and returns the envelope quickly to her pocket. But the con artist is very shrewd, she has short-changed the cashier one dollar, and the cashier, thinking that he is on to her, finds it. The cashier tells the con artist that she is short one dollar. The con artist pretends to be flustered and very embarrassed. She says that she will have to go home or back to the office or out to her car or whatever and get the additional one dollar. She takes back the original bills and change and gives the clerk an envelope, in which the clerk thinks the twenty dollar bill has been deposited, and tells him to keep that in the register until she returns with the one dollar that she owes him. It may be hours before the clerk opens the envelope and discovers that the con artist has left an envelope with a blank piece of paper inside.

The Shell Game

No one knows exactly when the shell game was introduced to the American public but it has probably been played for hundreds of years. It was a popular pastime among the 49ers in California when they were digging for gold. By the turn of the century it had returned to the cities and was causing the police of Chicago so much trouble that they printed descriptions of the game in the newspapers to warn the public. But this only increased the shell men, or nut men as the press called them, and didn't discourage the suckers from the rural parts of America, who never read the big city newspapers anyway.

The way con artists operate the shell game is very simple. Three half shells of a walnut, a rubber pea, two milk crates, and a small table or even a large piece of cardboard complete the con artists's outfit. However, at least one booster (or shill) is essential to the success of the swindle. The shell game is played as follows:

1. The operator of the con game hides the pea under one walnut shell. Then, he moves the shells around the table and bets that no one can tell which shell the pea is under. The booster (or shill), who dresses differently than the con artist, is the first one up to play the game. It is very important that the con artist running the game looks slightly less affluent than the people in the area and that the booster dresses almost exactly like the people in the area.
2. The booster will come up to the game, and the con operator, with ease and carelessness (which only appears to be carelessness), allows the pea to slide slowly underneath one of the shells. This motion is seen by the onlookers. The booster makes a bet and, of course, wins, so the true victim is drawn into the game.
3. The operator appears to handle the shells more carelessly than before. He allows the pea to remain for an instant under the edge of one of the shells. The victim sees this and imagines that he has a sure thing. He makes his bet and picks up the shell only to find it empty. The shell operator, skilled in handling the pea, causes it to pass under the shell picked up by the victim and inside the next shell. This motion is too quick for detection.

Some of the old-time shell game operators were real artists in the truest sense of the word. Not only were their fingers trained to a degree of deftness rarely seen today, but their shtick or spiel was so hypnotic in its effect on suckers that, had they gone on stage with these talents, many of them would have earned far more fame and more fortune than they did as con artists and sidewalk swindlers.

The key to success in this game is to have crowds, crowds, crowds, because they have money, money, money. On the streets of New York at any given time you can see thousands of these shell game operators working the streets and sidewalks. What makes this game so enticing to tourists and people who do not know about it is the fact that crowds are lured into it. The operator counts on the crowds and their noise.

The booster will scream exuberantly that he has won ten, twenty, fifty or a hundred dollars, thereby attracting a crowd. As we all know, people like to know what's going on to attract a crowd. So, what do we do? We go to the head of the crowd to see what is going on, see the money that is being exchanged, see how easy it is to win (at least for the booster), and offer to give it a shot. The suckers get caught up in the fast pace and large crowds involved in these games.

The police frequently are asked by local merchants to move these con artists along, as they create such crowd problems that regular customers can't enter a store. When the police are seen coming down the block, either with their sweep vans or on foot patrol, the shell game operator simply packs up his milk crates, stuffs his cardboard box into one of the milk crates, drops his lucky pea into his pocket and moves on. Usually, his shop is set up another thirty feet down the block.

Three Card Monte

Three Card Monte may not be as old as the shell game but it is every bit as popular. You encounter it most often today among people waiting for buses, trains and planes. Wherever people have time to kill, a Three Card Monte operator finds enough suckers to make the time profitable for her. This game is similar to the shell game, the only difference being three playing cards instead of walnut shells and a pea.

For instance, if three aces are used—hearts, spades and clubs—they are shuffled around the table in the same manner as the shells and the operator invites the onlookers to pick out the ace of clubs. If she operates with a shill (or booster), she will allow the shill to win a few bets to gain the confidence of the crowd. Sometimes the confederate is given an opportunity to mark the cards so that everybody but the operator knows which one is marked.

After the shill and some of the outsiders win a few bets on the marked card someone is induced to put up a really big bet. But when the sucker turns up the marked card it is not the ace of clubs but the ace of spades. Obviously this is a good example of palming and the game should really be called Four Card Monte. Certainly, four cards are involved though the sucker doesn't know it.

Three Card Monte has many variations, but the best that we have ever seen was worked by a sole operator who used to hang around Penn Station in New York City. He used no marked cards, no shills and he paid off when he lost; after all, he had a two to one advantage so he could plan on winning two-thirds of the time. But to make doubly sure he won, he had a way of shuffling the cards flat on the table that confused anybody who tried to keep his eye on the right card.

Bank Con Artists

Not many years ago, and within the memory of many people, a person who wanted to open a checking account was required to furnish references and one of them was expected to be some type of bank reference. Things are different today. Bankers, pressured by competition and statistics, open checking accounts without any investigation of the applicant or verification of his or her claims to previous banking and business connections. The pressure of competition is obvious; there are almost as many banks as there are drugstores, more banks than bookstores, and their advertising has changed from being institutional to being modern and slick. They spend more money advertising for new accounts than they lose on bad ones. What they don't take into consideration is that their advertising invites swindlers.

There is an old saying among bank management: "Strangers are not always crooks, but crooks are usually strangers." The most common type of bank swindle by con artists is the split deposit con. Many times a con will open an account under a fictitious name and place a small amount of money in the account, usually fifty to a hundred dollars. After the account is opened, they receive various paperwork and documentation. Frequently, the con will visit the bank making small deposits of ten or fifteen dollars or depositing a check for fifty dollars and asking for twenty dollars cash back. This is to build up the confidence of the people in the bank so that he or she is easily recognized as being a bank customer.

One of Joe's investigations involved a woman, who through a split deposit transaction, deposited a check at her bank for $7,550. She deposited $4,050 to her account and asked for cash back in the amount of $3,500. At another bank she obtained $3,650 cash in a similar transaction. The following Monday, she cashed checks on her accounts for $1,500 at each bank. The total take for one week was $10,150, which is not too bad when you consider that most people do not make that in six months.

The split deposit scam is very easy to do because it plays on the confidence of the teller. When a teller sees that a person is depositing a check for around seven thousand dollars into an account and is only asking for a portion back, they presume the check will be good. But, the con artist knows the check is worthless and that the bank will discover this at the end of the day when they do their tally. The key to this con is the check *must not* be drawn on the bank being swindled.

Many smart con artists know that a bank manager has to initial a check for a large amount before it can be cashed. What they do is scope out the bank to learn the manager's name and, therefore, his initials. They forge the manager's initials on the check and then present the check to the teller at the busiest time of the day. The teller usually will cash the check without question.

The con artist's success depends on his or her ability to appear normal. The job of selecting surnames for use in a bank scam is also a serious undertaking. The names picked should usually fit the racial characteristics of the con artist. Some names repeatedly used in bank scams are Daley, Ferguson, Ford, Hart, Marlowe, Martin, Mansfield, Mellon, Payne, Robinson, Sheppard, Taylor and Wilson. When a banker meets a person using a familiar surname by right or by choice he is inclined to be more than usually pleased to serve him. In banking, to be more than usually pleased means to freely accommodate the person with any services needed. These names appear to have an actual psychological effect upon those who see or use them.

Swindlers not blessed with an honest face can make good use of a uniform. The uniform might be that of an armed service, a civic organization or commercial enterprise. For several years banks in our area have been plagued by a person who masquerades as a filling station employee while negotiating worthless checks. By disguising himself in an oil-stained uniform, generally bearing a major oil company's insignia, he leads bank tellers to believe that he is employed locally and has been sent to the bank simply to cash his employer's checks. These are from a number of banks all bearing different signatures and all made out to the station that he pretends to represent. His average take at each bank was five hundred to seven hundred and fifty dollars.

Several checks stolen from a steel company were cashed at various stores by con artists in work clothes and steel helmets. In another case, checks stolen from a nursing home were cashed by a woman in an immaculate nurse's uniform.

But the key to these types of bank swindles is that the con artists must make themselves familiar to the people employed by the bank, either by frequently walking in and making minor deposits or by going into the bank with an appearance, name and uniform so that they appear to be nothing other than the average Joe simply trying to deposit a paycheck and take a little bit home for his week's wages.

The Free Inspection Con

Whatever your profession or business, the free inspection con is the simplest come-on for a profitable fraud. TV repairmen, auto mechanics, heating and air conditioning engineers, insect and rodent exterminators make the offer for a free inspection by advertising or by door-to-door canvassing. Once inside the TV set, under the automobile or under the house, the most cursory examination will disclose numerous components that need repair or replacing.

If a homeowner has been dumb enough to mail a postage-free return postcard on which he has indicated an interest in having, let's say, his furnace inspected, a smart operator may knock on his door and intimate that he represents a city government agency or utility company and request permission to inspect the home heating plant. The typical procedure of the furnace repair con is to gain access to the heating plant by some ruse and then take it apart and make it so that it will not be operable. At that point the con can refuse to assemble the parts into working condition on the grounds that the furnace is in immediate danger of causing a fire or explosion or of giving off deadly gas fumes.

Dead Man's Curse Con

Sad but true, the obituary columns present another opportunity for con artists. If you or I happen to be one of those listed in the obituary, we do not have to worry about being victimized, do we? The obituary columns of newspapers provide endless sucker lists for a variety of swindles. Packages of worthless merchandise "ordered by the deceased" are delivered COD to the next of kin. Or the bereaved are notified that the deceased had an insurance policy with one premium still unpaid. "Just pay the $35 premium and the insurance check will be sent to you by return mail," states the con artist, but the money never is because the policy never was.

Heir hunters are still around too. People with fairly common surnames get letters every day telling them about the death in some distant city of a relative who left a sizable estate. The suckers are asked to identify themselves and send ten or fifteen dollars as a filing fee, "So that you can be put on the list to be paid." The filing fee goes directly into the con artist's pockets.

The Bank Examiner Fraud

The bank examiner fraud is a swindle based on the hidden desire of many people to serve as a secret agent for the police. Victims are located through telephone books or through surveys. The first telephone call to the victim is double-talk alleging that there is some problem with their account at the local bank. The next call is allegedly from an officer of the bank. The spiel is that one of the bank's employees has been tampering with the accounts of depositors, and they want to catch him, but they need the victim's help to do so.

Cooperative victims are then informed that they should simply go to the bank, withdraw a specific sum, usually just short of the victim's total deposited funds and bring it home. The victim is assured that the withdrawal will be secretly watched by an armed agent who will follow the victim home to make certain the money is safe.

A few minutes after arrival at home with the money, the victim is visited by the con artist posing as the armed agent. After some more double-talk, the swindler counts the victim's money, gives her a signed deposit slip and takes the money. Hours, days and even weeks later the victim finds out the name on the deposit slip is fictitious, the bank knows nothing of this employee, and the money given to the swindler is a total loss.

The Ponzi Scheme

The Ponzi scheme or kiting is the basis of all investment frauds, security frauds or get-rich-quick schemes. In a Ponzi scheme—named after Charles Ponzi, the American legend who in December 1919 started this scam—the swindler uses money invested by new victims to pay a high interest on the investments of earlier victims. The money from the earlier victims was appropriated for the operator's own use rather than investing it as claimed in the spiel. A Ponzi scheme collapses when the swindler runs out of victims.

The most common version of a Ponzi scheme are chain letters and pyramid sales schemes, but the swindle can take an infinite variety of subtler forms. Virtually any investment vehicle can start out legitimately and turn into a variation on Ponzi's original.

In recent years investigations have revealed that con artists have worked Ponzi operations in everything from offshore mutual and private hedge funds to real estate commodities contracts and gold coins. Hundreds of small investors around New York City were recently stung by a Los Angeles crook who sold them some $9 million worth of 270-day notes presumably invested in real estate and guaranteeing returns of 20 to 30 percent interest. Instead, the $9 million vanished.

A very juicy scandal uncovered within recent memory was the Home Stakes Production Company swindle. Home Stakes, based in Tulsa, Oklahoma, purported to be an oil drilling company run by an Oklahoma lawyer named Robert S. Trippet. Home Stakes sold tax shelter partnerships to hundreds of wealthy investors eager to avoid paying taxes. To disguise the complete lack of oil drilling operations, Trippet and his cronies fooled investors with a variety of maneuvers, even going so far as to paint irrigation pipes orange to make a California vegetable farm look like an operating oil field. When the company went bankrupt in 1973, unsuspecting investors lost $100 million or more. The list of investors was astounding and included some of the biggest names in United States industry, finance, law and show business. Some of the show business crowd victimized were Barbra Streisand, Liza Minelli, Walter Matthau, Candice Bergen, Bob Dylan, Mia Farrow, Barbara Walters and the late Jack Benny. Andy Williams alone was sunk for $538,000. So, those who get taken by a Ponzi racket have one consolation: They can always boast that they are in the same league with the nation's financial elite.

Our experience has shown that these Ponzi swindlers proliferate in cyclical patterns throughout history and very often take place when inflation and unemployment are very high. There is never a shortage of suckers ready to take a tumble. What sets Ponzi schemes apart from other more intricate swindles is this: The money the investors put up isn't invested in anything, and the profits are paid out of new money from subsequent investors. Eventually there aren't enough newcomers to keep this snowball going, and the game collapses.

No one knows if a successful Ponzi operator has ever found a way to close-out his swindle without it collapsing. When a Ponzi scheme collapses all of the latecomers lose. Only early investors can win, but many of them lose, too, because they reinvest with the expectation of making larger and larger gains. They become trapped by their own greed. To profit from a Ponzi fraud it's not enough to be the first one in; you have to be the first one out as well.

Bunko Games

The pigeon drop or pocketbook drop is the street bunko game that requires the minimum number of props: a pocketbook or an envelope and a sizable amount of cash. The pigeon is the victim and no more than two or three swindlers participate in the crime.

The game begins in the presence of the potential victim, when one of the swindlers apparently finds a pocketbook or envelope filled with money, usually from $500 to $2,500. The approach to the victim is disarming, combining happiness in finding the money along with the question, "What do I do now?" As the victim starts to discuss the swindler's apparent good fortune, a second swindler shows up. Assuming the roll of a stranger who just happens to witness the find and wants to be part of it, the second swindler joins in the spiel that makes the victim a partner in a plan to hold the money until the origin of the cash can be determined.

Since this will take time, the two swindlers team up to convince the sucker that he should hold the funds, but to assure them of the victim's good faith, they ask him to show cash equal to the amount found or close to it. Faced with the possible loss of one-third of the money, the gullible victim goes to a bank, gets the cash and shows it to the swindlers. They go through the motions of counting it, advising the victim of their satisfaction. They bundle the found money with the victim's cash, hand it to him, and arrange to meet again the next day.

Sometime after this parting, the natural curiosity of the victim leads to an examination of the secret bundle of money. It turns out to be newspapers or regular plain paper cut to money size. The swindlers switched the bundle just before they parted from the victim.

Swindles Against the Elderly

On the bottom of any detective's list of social miscreants would be the con man who impersonates a Social Security employee to gain access to an elderly person's home and confidence. Once this relationship is established there are a variety of con games used by these individuals. Here are a few along with actual case histories from the files of the Social Security Administration.

We once investigated two con men who contacted Social Security recipients, two elderly females, aged eighty-six and eighty-four, and told them that there had been overpayment. The eighty-six-year-old woman turned over $7,050 to the impersonators. The eighty-four-year-old told them she didn't have the $1,628 demanded, but that she could have it for them the next day. She then called the Social Security Office. This matter was reported to the Federal Bureau of Investigation.

Another type of con, frequently targeted toward elderly men, are pills and devices to enhance sex and advertised in senior citizen magazines or by direct mail. It is quite easy to purchase mailing lists, which go into great demographic detail in a market area. For instance, if a person wanted to target males over age sixty who reside in a certain location, they would simply contact a mailing label company who would ship them thousands of labels compiled according to recent research data. Armed with this information, con artists target these individuals and offer them pills and juices that they say can make a man, regardless of age, romantic, young, potent, as virile as the gods. These products are sold for ten to twenty dollars, but are made of nothing but pineapple, papaya, peach, grape and apple juice.

Another con involving the elderly is the dance studio scam. In the most prominent one, the slick con artist preys on the desire of elderly widows and spinsters for attention and the emotional satisfaction this brings to an otherwise lonely existence. Swindling in this area is made possible through the device of lifetime memberships, whereby a studio contracts to provide several thousand hours of instruction to an elderly person who pays in advance. Many victims that we have met have reported to the Better Business Bureau that they have been bilked out of their life's savings for a lifetime membership or multiple lifetime memberships. In one case a dance studio signed a sixty-nine-year-old widow to eight lifetime memberships entitling her to 3,100 hours of instruction at a cost of $34,913.00. She was promised attractive male dancing partners and was assured that the lessons would make her a gifted dancer so that she could perform on television.

Another type of swindle is called the lonely hearts club. What these operators do is try to offer personal introductions to members of the opposite sex. They do not deliver people and charge anywhere from fifty to two hundred dollars. After responding to a newspaper ad for a matchmaker service for the elderly, the subscriber will call to investigate, send in his payment, and then wait patiently for his perfect match to show up. He is told over the telephone to exercise patience while the vast staff of the club sort out the right person for the match. In essence, this elderly victim is contacting one or two people working in a room with nothing but two phone lines and two chairs!

There are also correspondence clubs that take the initial deposits and then go much further to receive more funds from their cons. An elderly gentleman receives delightful letters from a widow across the country found for him by the correspondence club. These, of course, are form letters that are written by the thousands each month by the employees of the scam. After a few months of writing, the widow declares her intentions to visit the gentleman. His interest peaked, he is all set for this visit. However, in transit to the gentleman's home, she falls seriously "ill" and cables him for a bundle of money just until she can get to her own bank and make a withdrawal. The money is sent by the expectant gentleman and that is the last that is heard of the nonexistent widow.

Gypsy swindlers and door-to-door confidence men exploit the elderly to the tune of millions annually through a variety of schemes. Many of these con artists pose as city inspectors telling people that their storm sewers need cleaning to pass inspection. They will work two hours and charge a person $1,050. Other times they will insist that they are roofing inspectors and state that the roof will need painting and repair. They will go on the roof and work for about three or four hours and charge $1,685.

In another investigation that we handled, a retired physician in his eighties gave a representative of an alleged termite control firm $1,790 for treatment of his home, after being shown a piece of termite-eaten wood supposedly removed from his basement. Subsequent investigation failed to establish that there was any termite activity in the home.

A Glossary for Con Artists

Noted below is the compendium of con artist language. Be sure con artists in your works are flamboyant, extraverted and expert salesmen. To make them realistic you should have them use the following terms and know exactly what they mean:

Big Con *A confidence game or trick, usually with an elaborate set up, that nets the swindler big money.*

Boob *A victim or dupe.*

Booster *A shoplifter, also an assistant to the operator of a con game.*

Bunko *A confidence game or swindle.*

Cannon *A pickpocket.*

Capper *An outside man who works for a gambler, one who brings in the suckers.*

Century *A one hundred dollar bill, also called a C-note.*

Check Kiting *Passing a check whose amount has been fraudulently raised. A check bearing a forged signature or check without funds to cover it.*

Chump *A sucker.*

Clip Artist *A swindler.*

Cold Deck *A deck of cards dishonestly introduced into a game.*

Flush *Describes a sucker who has plenty of money.*

Front Money *Money put up to lead a sucker into a swindle.*

Gaff *Any method, device or system used by a swindler to trick a sucker.*

Grand *A thousand dollars or G-note.*

Gyp Artist *A swindler.*

Haul *The swindler's take or profit, also called loot, gravy, cut, doe or swag.*

Hooked *To be swindled.*

Laying Paper *Passing worthless checks.*

Layout *The swindler's paraphernalia, also called the set up.*

Mark *A prospective or actual victim of a confidence game.*

Nut *The sum total of expenses.*

One Spot *A one dollar bill.*

Paper Hanger *A bad check passer.*

Patsy *A dupe or victim of a swindle.*

Phony *Counterfeit money or a package of paper with good bills on the outside.*

Pigeon *The dupe or victim of a confidence game.*

Poke *A pocketbook or wallet.*

Rap *A complaint or criminal charge.*

Salesman *A swindlers advanceman who makes the first contact with the mark.*

Score *To pull off a swindle and then the proceeds from the swindle.*

Shill *A swindler's assistant who poses as one of the crowd. He may be permitted to win a short card game to facilitate bringing in victims.*

Short Con *A confidence game in which little preparation is needed and small stakes are involved.*

Spieler *The person who does most of the talking in a con game.*

Steerer *A confidence operator who first approaches the intended victim. Also called the salesman.*

Sucker *From the swindler's standpoint any person not engaged in some swindling activity. Also called the fall guy, sap, pigeon, dupe, gull, easy mark, boob, chump, egg, patsy or customer.*

Thimble Rigger *A shell game operator.*

Touch *The victim of a swindle or a sucker.*

Trick *A swindle. To pull a trick is to swindle.*

Trim *To swindle, fleece, jip, clip, beat or cheat a sucker.*

F I V E

Counterfeiters and Forgers

We all know that the most desirable article to forge is paper money. But, counterfeiters and forgers do not just deal in currency. Anything that can be used to make a profit will be duplicated and sold: artwork, bank checks and stocks and bonds, even blue jeans and pocketbooks. If there is a market for an item, you can almost guarantee there will be someone willing to reproduce it cheaper.

What is counterfeiting? It is defined in criminal codes as an act of copying or producing a genuine facsimile for the purpose of unlawfully circulating them for profit. The enforcement of federal counterfeiting laws is done mainly by the U.S. Treasury Department through the Secret Service.

Currencies

The currency most often counterfeited in the U.S. is the twenty dollar bill. Store clerks will take them with little or no hesitation; especially when a cashier is confronted with a line of customers. Today's counterfeiters will not attempt to fool the unsuspecting cashier with a perfectly manufactured counterfeit bill. Instead, they rely on the clerk's lack of attention to pass the bogus bills. This is achieved by placing the counterfeit currency between a number of authentic bills, and by asking a number of complicated questions so the checkout line stacks up with angry customers who preoccupy the cashier.

Modern Money

We have all seen in the movies the master engraver. The typical scene is a small, dimly lit room, perhaps tucked away in a basement or to the rear of a small curio shop in a seedy part of town. The engraver sits on a stool, hunched over a small wooden bench table. One light fixture hangs over the table. His sleeves are rolled up and a visor is on top of his head shading his eyes from the harsh light. A tiny razor-sharp chisel is used to precisely and meticulously carve into a metal plate the image of a one hundred dollar bill. Once both sides of the bill are complete, the plates are placed into a press and one at a time these one hundred dollar bills are reproduced.

This is not the norm today. Small-time hoods duplicate currency on high-quality color copy machines that cost in excess of $80,000 each, or computers with laser printers. Unlike the master engraver, anyone with little or no art skills can make a high-quality reproduction of U.S. currency. Counterfeiters use high-tech software programs to accomplish this. Not all the counterfeit monies produced today are from professional criminals. School-aged children use their library copiers to reproduce money to buy items from their cafeteria vending machines. More gutsy juveniles will attempt to make purchases at a local convenience store with photocopied money.

Worth the Paper and Ink

The paper used to make genuine U.S. currency is 100 percent cotton rag that holds a unique textured surface. This texture can be easily observed and felt when it is handled. Small red and blue fibers are embedded in the paper. The paper used for currency is very tightly controlled, making it almost impossible to obtain. One enterprising counterfeiter, knowing of the tiny red and blue fibers, attempted to duplicate the paper by carefully gluing tiny bits of red and blue fiber onto his counterfeit money.

The United States government is now taking steps to stop the ease of duplicating its currency. Beginning in 1996, United States currency will contain a number of new security characteristics. Some of these characteristics will be kept secret for security reasons, but basically they are going to have some of the same features found in currency in European countries. The currency will contain watermarks that will only be visible when looked at with lighting behind the currency itself. This is designed to eliminate the possibility of copying currency with a copy machine, because these watermarks will not transfer. Another protection from copiers or high-quality laser printers will be the introduction of microprinting. Microprinting is impossible to reproduce through photocopying because the tiny characters blur when photocopied.

The standard red and blue fibers will be placed in different locations that will indicate the denomination of the currency. The green ink, which is also a tightly controlled product, will still be used, but this new currency will have an additional ink that will change colors when viewed at different angles.

Credit Card Fraud/Counterfeiting

It's actually pretty simple to get credit card numbers. A search of apartment building dumpsters for sales receipts or billing account statements will yield a motherlode of information. Carbon copies thrown in retail outlet dumpsters is another method, and, of course, a salesman looking to make a fast buck is also a good source for charge card numbers.

Credit card information is also easily obtained through telemarketing scams. Basically, you receive a telephone call stating that you won an outstanding prize or the vacation of your dreams. The only problem is that for you to receive your prize, you first have to satisfy your tax obligation or a shipping fee for your prize to be delivered. One method suggested to you is paying with your Visa or MasterCard. Once the number is obtained, it is then imprinted on a bogus charge card.

These bogus charge cards are either manufactured, usually in a well-organized and equipped print shop, or stolen with inside help from the company of issue. The charge card can now easily be used for at least thirty days, which is the usual billing cycle, without threat of apprehension.

Counterfeit losses have generally represented a small percentage of volume loss for the major bank credit card companies—Visa and MasterCard International. These credit card vendors paid the problem scant attention until the involvement of organized crime and the rising losses. MasterCard lost $172,000 to counterfeiters in 1979, but $9.3 million in 1983 on a total of $41.8 billion dollars in sales. The $9.3 million is not tremendous, but the growth is alarming. According to Visa, 93 percent of U.S. counterfeiting occurs in twelve states, and card fraud operations appear to coincide with the locations of major, known organized crime families. It has been determined that 82 percent of all counterfeit and altered card transactions took place in New York, New Jersey and Florida.

Lost or stolen cards are used first for large purchases by criminals. Counterfeiting and alterations are usually the second step for a stolen card. When the issuer finally hotlists the account number, counterfeiters recycle their cards using methods ranging from the crude—cutting the numbers off and pasting them on another card—to the sophisticated—$140,000 embossing machines.

Today, there are basically three types of counterfeit cards being used: Kimble Stolen Plastic, Silkscreen and Lithographs.

Kimble Stolen Plastic

Kimble cards are the Bank of America cards that were taken in an armed robbery in 1981; they are named after the executive who made the cards at Bank of America. These cards are perfect because they are embossed with valid names and account numbers, and are difficult to detect as counterfeits because the card is flawless. These cards can be detected as counterfeit after they are embossed by the following irregularities:

1. Some will have small square outlines around the letters or the name. This is because the same embossing pressure was applied on the letters as the numbers.
2. All Kimble stolen cards counterfeited to date have no star. The Bank of America star has five points, but counterfeiters are embossing a six-point star that looks like a daisy flower. Some cards have been recovered with a dot in place of the star.

The only positive way to tell if the card is a Kimble stolen card is to photocopy the back with the signature panel (for the signature record), then scrap off the center with a sharp knife. If the number 03 781-7-81-682 appears under the panel, this card is a Kimble counterfeit.

Kimble counterfeit cards will not have any information recorded on the magnetic stripe on the back of the card. Valid Bank of America cards will contain the following information in the magnetic stripe: card number, name of the cardholder, expiration date, number of valid cards issued, and the reason for re-issue. Counterfeiters have digital machinery that can match the magnetic strip to the card.

Silkscreens

Here are some ways to identify counterfeit credit cards that have been created using silkscreening:

1. They are always on blank white plastic cards.
2. The pin code is very smooth and even looking.
3. The edges of the letters are jagged like sawed teeth. This can be detected with a magnifying glass.
4. You can feel the paint on the smooth plastic. This is due to criminals using the wrong type and mixture of paint. Valid cards are sprayed front and back with

clear plastic, this gives the card a shiny appearance. Altered cards will contain air bubbles in the plastic, which can be detected by scrutinizing the card.

5. The edges of the card are rough because of the way they were cut. The roughness can be detected with a magnifying glass. Valid cards are always smoothly cut.

Lithographs

1. They are made on white plastic sheets.
2. Irregularities in the paint texture and color are due to using the wrong type and mixture of paint. The paint color is dotted or uneven, which can be detected by using a magnifying glass.
3. The faintness in the detail of the card is caused by the wrong amount of heat applied to the plate when burned. Normally the plate is burned with a 2,000- or 4,000-watt lamp for two to four minutes. Direct sunlight can also be used to burn the plate, but this is hit or miss.
4. Cards are sprayed with clear plastic to give it a shiny appearance. When this is done you can see air bubbles on the card by carefully scrutinizing the card.
5. When the card is embossed some of the paint will fall off the numbers and the letters. This happens because the card was not covered with clear plastic.

Signature Panels

Signature panels can be altered in two ways:

1. By covering the old panel with a false one made of glued-on paper, adhesive tape, white paint or white fingernail polish. To detect these alterations one must examine the panel closely. If the panel has been damaged or is missing this could indicate an altered card. False panels often show other signs of alteration: paper or tape panels may have edges that can be lifted off, paint or nail polish panels are easily chipped and may show brush marks or light erasures. Often the edges of altered panels are irregular.

2. A mixture of red wine vinegar and rubbing alcohol, ninety percent vinegar and ten percent alcohol, will erase the signature without damaging the plastic.

To write consistently and accurately concerning credit card fraud, you must have a suitable definition of terms used by the industry and criminals in these enterprises:

Credit card *A plastic card empowering the holder to buy or borrow against credit established by the issuer. Funds spent are charged to the cardholder's account. The cardholder is then billed at a later date.*

Bank credit cards *A card issued by a bank offering revolving extended credit to the cardholder. The cardholder has the choice to pay in full to save interest charges or to pay a lesser amount and have interest charged on the outstanding balance. A cash advance can also be obtained, and interest is charged from the day the cash is received.*

Travel and entertainment cards *A travel and entertainment card (commonly referred to as a T&E card) provides credit between purchase and billing, at which time the cardholder is expected to settle the account balance. A charge is also made to the merchant calculated on the value of sales made with this card. Examples of this type of card are American Express and Diner's Club.*

Retailer cards *A retailer card is commonly referred to as an in-house or in-store card and is issued by or on behalf of merchants. It is generally used only at the merchant's outlet. An example of this is a Sears or a J.C. Penney's card.*

Gas and oil cards *A form of retailer charge card the use of which is usually restricted to the purchase of gasoline, diesel fuel oil and accessories.*

Debit card *A debit card is an instrument of payment that can be used to obtain cash, goods and services and is linked to the cardholder's bank account. A debit card is different* *from a credit card in that the cardholder's account is electronically debited at the time of the transaction. There is no credit. An example of this type of debit card is the MAC or Plus Cirrus cards, which enable you to make cash withdrawals at automatic teller machines at banks, convenience stores or supermarkets.*

Altered card *Initially a payment device that was manufactured by an authorized issuer but which was lost or stolen and re-embossed, re-fabricated or otherwise modified to reflect a name, account number, expiration date and/or signature other than that of the valid cardholder.*

Counterfeit cards *A payment device that has been printed, embossed and/or encoded to represent a valid card, but which is not valid because an issuer did not authorize its manufacture.*

White plastic card *A blank, credit card-sized piece of plastic embossed with a valid cardholder name, account number and expiration date. This card is to imprint a sales draft which is presented for payment to the institution that supposedly issued the card. The term white plastic is generic since the card may be of any color, including blue, white, gold and red.*

Authorization *A process by which approval for a transaction is required when the merchant accepts a card as a means of payment or when a financial institution accepts a card as a means of payment or of a cash disbursement.*

Card recovery bulletin *A list of account numbers (first published by Visa) that have been blocked from further use; this bulletin is referred to generically as the hot card list. It is used by most major credit card issuers.*

Cardholder *An individual to whom a credit card has been issued or one authorized to use such a card.*

Interchange *The exchange of paper between approved Visa and MasterCard members.*

Fraudulent application *An instrument containing false cardholder information upon which an issuer of a payment device relies for the extension of credit or debit accounts to a cardholder.*

Criminals of credit card fraud usually have certain qualities about them that should be reflected in your works:

1. The criminal will usually make indiscriminate purchases without regard to size, color, style or price. An example of this would be a criminal who would go into a stereo or audio-video store and immediately buy an expensive stereo system without listening to the speakers, looking at the placement of the woofer and tweeter or evaluating the power of the amplifier.

   Just imagine if you or I were to walk into a store and decide to spend one or two thousand dollars on a stereo system. We would usually ask to test a CD or cassette so we could listen to the different types of speakers on display. Slowly, we would settle on a few speakers that sounded good and we would eventually narrow our choice down to one set. Speakers are typically the most important part of a person's stereo system, and the component they are most selective about. Unfortunately, many salespeople who work on commission are eager to close a sale and will not question a person who comes in and quickly orders a large item without appearing to think about the purchase.

2. The criminal may instead be talkative or will delay a selection repeatedly until the clerk is upset. The reason for this is to make the clerk rush to close the sale and get rid of this annoying customer. This rush may keep the clerk from checking the signature on the sales slip with the one on the back of the card.

3. The criminal may also pose as a customer who appears just before quitting time. This is a very common tech-

nique that criminals use. Often times salespeople work ten- to fourteen-hour days and the last thing they want is to hassle with a sale (regardless of the commission) in the ten minutes before closing time. Both of us have experience in retail sales, and we know what it is like to be in a store for fourteen hours and to be trying to unwind at the end of the day with a cup of coffee or by taking a peek at the day's newspaper when a customer rushes in. Of course salespeople figure a late arrival is not a very serious customer and instead is simply rushing in to pick up a small accessory. The smart criminal will hurry a clerk at quitting time and thereby cause the clerk to not be as careful with checking the card.

4. Criminals often purchase large items such as a color television console and insist on taking the item immediately instead of having it delivered.
5. Criminals refuse alterations on wearing apparel even though the alterations are included in the selling price.
6. A customer making purchases, leaving the store with the merchandise and then returning to make additional purchases may be using a stolen card.
7. Criminals are sometimes customers who do not appear to be well dressed but who are purchasing expensive items.
8. A customer who pulls the credit card out of his pocket, not his wallet should raise suspicion. This is a common technique that is not usually caught by younger salespeople. However, the older and more experienced a salesperson, the more this is a tip off that the card is actually stolen.

Other Documentation

Money orders, traveler's checks, store coupons, stock and bond certificates and letters of credit can all be duplicated. The method is again the theft of an original, which is then duplicated on a copy machine or a personal computer system. Fraudulent stock and bond certificates are often used to obtain credit or a loan from a bank.

Marketable Goods

You name it, they make it. Whether it is the latest CD, videotape, or computer software program, it is probably being pirated somewhere. This could be performed in a small operation or in a large factory, often in a foreign country. This process is profitable because no royalties are paid, the inferior merchandise used is cheap to manufacture, there is no middleman, and they pay no taxes.

Basically, the item, which could be anything from a sneaker to a watch, is examined by a manufacturer. The duplicate will look the same as the originals, but will be made of the cheapest possible materials.

Forgery

Forgery is the alteration of a written document with the intent to defraud a person by representing the document as genuine. The alteration could be signing a blank check or reproducing the original and representing it as the original.

Literary Forgery

Counterfeiting manuscripts and other printed materials is a profitable business. William H. V. Ireland, who was taught the engraving business by his father, reproduced several Shakespearean pieces of literature. Ireland even wrote an entire play attributing it to Shakespeare. Eventually, Ireland told the world and even demonstrated how he manufactured the writings, which included making the inks, paper and Shakespeare's signature.

Most recently, the magazine *Stern*, which is published in West Germany, reported having obtained a number of diaries written by Adolf Hitler. This hoax was discovered through scientific laboratory analysis of the materials present in the diary, and testing by a highly-trained handwriting expert. The contents of the diary contained misinformation that was easily refuted by historians.

The ever-increasing demand for autographs of the famous, such as movie stars, national heroes and sports figures, generates high price tags. Autograph forgers will, through both artistic skill and practice, duplicate the signatures of the famous. When the autograph is from earlier times, the inks and the writing utensils must match the time period. Failure to use authentic inks and tools is one of the main reasons that unskilled forgers meet their demise.

Electronic Forgery

Electronic forgery is becoming commonplace. Money can be fraudulently transferred among bank accounts using computers. This is accomplished either by a bank employee or over telephone lines via a personal computer and modem. Some computer experts, known as hackers, attempt to gain entry into business accounts through their technical abilities. These hackers can even shield themselves from apprehension by using a network of nontraceable telephone extensions. Credit card numbers can also be obtained using computers. Credit card agencies which perform audits also aid the criminal in his endeavors, as an unscrupulous auditor will sell card numbers.

Art Forgery

When someone creates a replica of a piece of art, and then sells it claiming it is the original, he is committing forgery. The art of the masters has been forged with such skill that even the copies have been mistaken for authentic pieces and sold as originals.

To forge art, the forger must be a skilled artist himself. If it is a painting that is going to be forged, the forger must study the style of painting including brushstrokes, the way paints are made, the colors used, and even the way the canvas is prepared. The forgery must then be aged. One method to age a painting is to place it in an oven. Another method is to drill small holes into wood art to give the appearance of worm holes. Some forgers will even acquire a canvas dating back to the original period and then create their forgery by scraping off the original painting and painting the forgery on top.

Today, forged art items, especially rare pieces dating back to the seventeenth and eighteenth century or earlier, are easy to detect. Before the advances of modern laboratory analysis, an expert would have to examine the artwork and give his opinion as to whether or not the article was genuine. Modern laboratory analysis uses microscopes, X-rays, infrared, ultraviolet and even chemical analysis to detect the forger's handiwork. With an X-ray, you can look under the first layer of paint to see if there were previous paintings underneath. The use of infrared can reveal a signature that has been painted over by a forger who changed the signature to that of a famous artist.

By removing very small pieces of the paint found on the painting and analyzing those fragments, we can determine whether the pigments used were available during the period when the painting would have been completed. Through radio-carbon dating, organic material such as the wood used to construct the frame or the sculpture itself, can be dated. Also any paper or inks used to create the artwork can easily be dated based on the material content and the methods used to manufacture them.

Other Collectibles

Antique furniture, mechanical banks, porcelain curios, children's toys, clothing or anything else there's a market for, people are willing to forge. These items are easily aged by exposing them to moisture, harsh chemicals, rough handling, or outside elements, just to name a few. These collectibles can then be sold for high profits at swap meets, antique shows and even garage sales.

Coins. Forging coins can be extremely profitable. Coin collectors or numismatists are willing to pay high prices to add specific coins to their collections. Ancient coins from Europe are basically a chunk of flattened silver or gold stamped by an engraved seal. These coins could later be easily changed to a higher value by restamping. Eventually the two-sided coin was manufactured.

Counterfeiters can easily duplicate two-sided coins and make a profit by limiting the amount of gold and silver placed in them. This became so much of a problem that coin counterfeiters can receive the death penalty.

Slugs are pieces of metal the same size and weight of the coin they are representing. Slugs are made by machines that cut nonprecious metals like iron into circles. There are no other identifying marks or alterations made to them. They are sold for use at toll booths or vending machines, and sell for around a quarter of the value of an actual coin.

Stamps. Postage stamps can also yield a profit for the talented forger. Rare or extremely old postage stamps can be reproduced and sold at extremely high prices. To perform this type of stamp forgery, simple engraving equipment is needed. A "vertical camera," which is used to reproduce high quality pictures, posters or brochures, can be used to take an extremely detailed photograph of an authentic stamp. Once a negative is produced, a counterfeit can easily be manufactured with a printing press.

SIX

FENCING

Other chapters cover the modus operandi of burglars, con artists, hijackers, skyjackers and carjackers. All of these criminals take property that can be used in one of two ways:

1. For the criminal's own personal benefit, which is actually pretty rare.
2. For sale to a second party (a fence). The money from this sale is then used for the criminal's own purpose.

The problem of converting stolen goods into cash is solved by finding a suitable *fence*. The choice of a fence will depend on a number of factors, most importantly the character and the type of stolen goods and the underworld connections of the particular criminal. The tremendous surge of crime by addicts in recent years has brought about changes in the multi-million dollar fencing trade. Some addicts have taken to selling stolen property, such as jewelry, on the streets.

Fencing is a very difficult criminal charge to prove because the evidence against the fence is largely circumstantial. The accused fence usually has a legitimate business, and the testimony of criminals who conducted business with him is generally not viewed as credible by members of the jury. The activities of the criminal receiver or fence have to be documented in great detail.

The most amazing aspect of a fence's operation is that, despite being surrounded by the bottomfeeders of the criminal underworld, he is, except for the fact that he receives stolen property, basically crime free. He is almost never a drug, alcohol or gambling abuser, because these personal problems would severely impair his ability to run a business.

Fences and the Law

An accused fence is most often charged with receiving stolen property. The police know that the property is stolen. But how do they go about the laborious task of proving this in court? For an item to be proven stolen and for the fence to have knowledge that it is stolen, the following four elements must *always* be present:

1. The property actually fenced must, of course, be stolen. If a person down on his luck decides to trade in the sofa or television set for a ridiculously low price and the fence buys it, has the fence committed any crime? Of course not; the fence has taken advantage of someone who accepted a low price for an item that he felt was no longer important in his life. This could be a destitute person seeking quick cash or a person cleaning out his garage. There is never a crime if the property is not stolen.
2. The property, if it is stolen, must be *received* by the fence, and the property must be found in the possession of the fence. If the store or warehouse where the stolen property is found is owned and occupied only by the fence, then there is no problem proving this in a criminal investigation. However, the difficulty comes

when there is more than one occupant of the warehouse or office space. When interviewing four partners in a rental warehouse where stolen property was found, the investigator will get dizzy watching the fingers the criminals point at each other.

3. The fence must have known that the property was stolen. How do you prove this knowledge if the accused won't admit to it?
    - The astronomically low price the fence paid for the item. This does not, in and of itself, prove the property was stolen.
    - The person it was purchased from could never have been the legitimate owner.
    - It was not bought from a responsible person or from an established business.
4. The accused fence must have the intention to convert the property *to his own use*. The detective attempts to obtain any record of an effort by the fence to dispose of the property. The detective must give particular attention to any arrangements for the concealment of the stolen goods.

Police Stings

Police agencies use undercover sting operations to catch stolen goods rings. The police will set up a store front that appears to sell completely legitimate merchandise such as bicycles. The police spread rumors to their contacts throughout the neighborhood that the store is really a front for the purchase of stolen property. When this rumor circulates and criminals bring in stolen merchandise, they can be selective about the items they purchase. During a sting operation, the police will purchase many hundreds of stolen items, which are ultimately returned to their rightful owners.

Overall, these operations are highly successful in terms of arrests made and merchandise recovered. And they generally make money! For example, a sting operation buys, let's say, $300,000 to $400,000 in stolen merchandise, and another $200,000 is expended in salaries, equipment, rent and overhead. After the merchandise is recovered and sold at auction if it cannot be returned, it will net usually four to five times the actual price paid by the law enforcement agency during the operation of the undercover sting.

Types of Fences

The *lay fence* knowingly buys stolen property for personal consumption: a pickpocket or petty thief who steals credit cards, checks, money or money orders and uses them himself. A lay fence buys stolen property without the intent to resell it to persons and instead intends to use it for his own benefit.

The *occasional fence* buys stolen property for resale to other persons but does so infrequently.

The *professional fence* deals in stolen merchandise as his main occupation. The difference between the occasional fence and the professional fence can be slight and is based on the frequency of accepting and reselling stolen goods. This can most easily be determined by the area in which a fence operates. City fences are often professionals while suburban fences are more often occasional fences.

The amount of merchandise a professional fence buys is affected by a number of factors: the condition of the market in general; the amount of capital he has; the difficulty of securing the merchandise, including the measures he must take to protect himself; and his contact with potential buyers. Of all these factors, fluctuations in the general market have the most impact on the fence's purchases. Many other things affect the business, such as the competence of the fence, his business sense, the attention he gives to his work, his particular industry or purchasing area, the condition of his health, his relationship with his wife, his personal and interpersonal relationships with thieves and the third party purchasers of his merchandise, and his professionalism in general.

What are the criteria that distinguish a fence from other traders in stolen goods?

First, the fence must be a dealer in stolen property: A buyer and seller with direct contact with thieves (sellers) and customers (buyers).

Second, the fence must be successful: He must buy and sell stolen property regularly and profitably and must have done so for a considerable period of time, usually many years.

Third, the fence must be public: He must acquire a reputation as a successful dealer in stolen property among police officers, thieves and others acquainted with the criminal community. He must eat, live, sleep and breath stolen property.

How to Become a Professional Fence

A fence does not become a fence overnight. Let's face it, anyone can make money buying and selling stolen property. But, a fence is a businessman, and, as such, he must have a little bit of capital, a little bit of opportunity, and willingness to do the work. As a businessman, the fence learns how to buy and sell merchandise, and where to locate his business so that it increases his capital. A fence starting out with minimal capital can overcome that hurdle with a willingness to look for opportunities to make a quick turnover. He must also have the ability to understand market conditions. There is a strong similarity between fences and entrepreneurs. For a fence to become successful he must gain as much knowledge as possible about the type of product that he is going to buy and sell.

The fence who is a generalist in all items is a ready market for those things most commonly stolen. He is much like a K mart or a WalMart of fences because his attraction is a wide variety of products. He will be willing to buy and sell most things without much notice. But, much like a regular business, he must be careful not to become overstocked.

Some fences specialize in one or two particular items such as art, antiques or jewelry, but most fences are generalists and can easily adapt to market conditions. The successful fence learns how to wheel and deal. He must examine

Who Came First?

It has been said many times that if there were no fences there would be no thieves. If there were no one to accept stolen property, burglars or thieves wouldn't steal. We can tell you that this is absolutely and unequivocally not true. Many thieves work without the aid of a fence, and others simply use the fence as a middleman.

For example: A burglar or thief steals money, credit cards or checks and passes them in retail establishments or through telephone orders. Some thieves sell stolen property to unsuspecting fences. In this particular instance, the fence becomes a noncriminal receiver of the property, as he has no idea that the merchandise is stolen. Also, even the most scrupulous and honest pawnbrokers, secondhand merchandise peddlers, auctioneers and junk dealers buy stolen property on occasion, that is, property that they *know* to be stolen.

If all fences were to disappear in the next three seconds, many thieves would shift to stealing merchandise that didn't need a fence to dispose of it. If there were no fences, there would still be all sorts of thieves and maybe some new kinds that we don't have now.

---

the ways that his property is bought and sold, paid for and transferred. A successful fence has the ability to make buying and selling stolen property appear no different from a normal, legitimate business. For example, a fence dealing in stolen automobiles will know a great deal about the laws governing registration, title searches, vehicle inspection, and transportation of vehicles.

The knowledge necessary to appear legitimate often comes from previous careers. A successful jewelry fence, for instance, is likely to be a former jeweler. A fence of stolen cars was once an automobile dealer. A fence of stolen art and antiques might be an artist himself. This is especially true when the fence deals exclusively in one type of commodity. But, a fence who is a generalist may employ specialists from time to time for merchandise such as art or jewelry.

Sooner or later, in order to go into business, the fence must go public, that is, become known to thieves, customers, police and others as a fence. Becoming public with the police involves getting questioned, investigated and searched; being handcuffed, booked, fingerprinted and photographed; facing a line-up; being brought before a judge, placed in a cell and bailed out; and of course, being officially and publicly known as a criminal. However, this can be beneficial to the fence, because within the criminal community an arrest or conviction is normally considered to be good evidence that the fence's relationship with the police is not too cozy and that he is not a rat—at least by the criminals' standards.

The most important part of being a successful fence is avoiding capture: The fence applies himself to buying and selling stolen property in such a way that makes him appear no different from other business owners. The most common way to do this is to accept stolen property as a supplement to a legitimate business such as a pawnshop, a consignment shop, or a used furniture or appliances store. It should also be remembered that unknowing legitimate businesses are sometimes used by criminals as fences. A good sob story can help a convincing thief unload a "hot" item to an unsuspecting mom and pop pawnshop.

Depicting a Professional Fence

The fence must have genius, that is, ingenuity, cunning, resourcefulness, energy and a mysterious power, sometimes referred to as personal magnetism or charisma. He must be able to manipulate thieves, because he depends on them to be profitable.

Like con men, the fences characterized in your works should be colorful and flamboyant. Basically their character has a lot to do with the way they negotiate, and negotiate they will! Who else could convince a con man to take $30 for $300 worth of retail goods? In addition to being flamboyant and charismatic, fences are outgoing, gregarious and knowledgeable of retail and wholesale prices.

So remember, when writing about fences, make them smart, colorful, flamboyant entrepreneurs and, of course, successful! Place them in legitimate businesses, in cities, in the suburbs, make them black or white, cooperative with the police investigators, but keep them one step ahead of the police. Make them wheelers and dealers, and good listeners, but most importantly make them stand out, so that they will be remembered in your works.

S E V E N

HOMICIDE

Criminal homicide occurs when the death of a human being is purposely, knowingly and/or recklessly caused by another. To make a charge of criminal homicide, the detective must first prove that a homicide actually occurred.

Medical Examiners

The forensic detective investigates a criminal homicide to determine the *manner* of death (the circumstances surrounding a death), while the medical examiner or coroner will determine the *cause* of death (the medical reason for death). The medical examiner or coroner will determine that death was due to homicide, suicide, an accident or a medical condition. A medical examiner must be a medical doctor, preferably a forensic pathologist. But a coroner, in some states, is not required to have a medical degree; they can be a Justice of the Peace, funeral director, a political appointee, or elected official.

As early as A.D. 1250 societies took action to apprehend and punish a person for taking the life of another intentionally. In China, the first documented mention of an autopsy listed how postmortem examinations should be conducted. It gave details on how a person's body should appear if he were involved in a drowning or a fire and explained the difference between blunt object wounds and stab wounds. The Chinese were also the first to use fingerprints to document people.

One of the first noted medical examiners in history was Antistius, the physician who examined the body of Julius Caesar. Antistius determined the cause of death to be one stab wound to Caesar's chest. He further documented that Caesar received twenty-three stab wounds at the hands of his assailant.

Autopsies developed in Europe around 1507. The first recorded coroner's examination in the United States was in New Plymouth, New England, around 1635, based on autopsies practiced in England.

Once it has been determined what killed a person, it is up to the detective to determine how and why a person died. And, of course, *who*donit.

Killing and the M.O.

When someone commits a crime, whether it's stealing a car or killing a person, the M.O. will change from scene to scene but remain consistent in other forms. Let's follow a homicide detective trying to make sense out of a series of killings that bear similar yet different traits.

Victim #1

Victim #1 was found dumped in a secluded wooded area and buried in a shallow grave with his hands tied with a small piece of clothes line. His mouth was filled with a piece of cloth, with another tied securely over the mouth and around the back of the head. The victim had numerous stab wounds to the chest, and the body revealed significant amounts of pre-mortem injuries, especially defense-type wounds on the hands and arms. The defense wounds were from striking out at the murderer. No signs of sexual assault were found.

It was determined that the victim was abducted while walking home from a part-time job at a convenience store. All the victim's jewelry and money were found on the body.

Victim #2

The second victim was again a male (about the same age as Victim #1) and had his hands bound with duct tape. A piece of duct tape was securely fastened over his mouth. The victim showed no signs of a struggle and had been strangled. Upon examining the body further, it was evident that he had been sexually assaulted and his neck chain was missing. The victim in this case was found dumped in the same area near the first victim.

Given this minimal amount of information, do you see a similar M.O.? The first victim was found with his hands secured with rope. The second was secured with duct tape. From this we can determine that our suspect exhibited *learned behavior*: While trying to secure the first victim, the suspect had problems, evidenced by the bruising on the hands and arms. This is also why he used duct tape on the mouth of the second victim.

The first victim was stabbed to death with the knife that was used to capture him. Our suspect lost control of the situation, and fearing apprehension, stabbed the victim. He panicked, drove the body to a remote wooded area, and disposed of the body. Our suspect intended to sexually assault the first victim, but because of the struggle and fear of detection, this did not occur.

The second victim was sexually assaulted and strangled and the necklace was removed. The second victim was more easily controlled; perhaps a handgun was used this time.

Shortly after or perhaps during the sexual assault, the victim was strangled. The chain was removed from the victim's neck, not for monetary gain, but to keep as a trophy, which our suspect may use in later sexual fantasies.

At first blush these two deaths seem only to be minimally related. But understanding and using the theory of learned behavior assists many detectives in apprehending suspects. By studying the crime scene, the detectives identify and interpret different pieces of evidence that can link one crime to another. Suspects with a long history of arrests and incarceration time change their M.O.'s as practice shows them what works and what doesn't.

Passion Killings

A passion killing usually takes place with little forethought and very little, if any, planning. An argument may begin over who takes out the trash, and the rage will become so intense that one person will lash out at the other. A physical assault will take place, and a weapon, if close at hand, will be used.

Domestic Assault

In a case where the assault takes place in a home, let's say in the kitchen, a knife or a large carving fork may be within easy reach. If there is a firearm in the house, the killer will seek it out and use it. The victim will be left at the scene, which will show signs of a struggle, but no attempt will be made to cover up the crime.

Homicide-Suicide

With jilted lovers, the rejected boyfriend will plan a meeting with his lover as a desperate last attempt at reconciliation. The meeting will be conducted in a semi-secluded area, such as a familiar park, perhaps a place that has special meaning to the couple. The man, on realizing that his attempts to reunite are not working, will pull out a weapon, usually a handgun, shoot his lover and then himself.

The Disgruntled Employee

We've heard a lot about disgruntled employees recently, most notably, stressed-out postal service workers who go into their former offices and begin shooting. A disgruntled employee is often distraught over the promotion of a co-worker or over being fired and usually plans revenge, including a hit list of people he wants to kill. He will obtain enough weaponry to complete his mission and then some. Once he has made up his mind, there is no stopping him. The killing spree will occur at the work place during working hours.

Premeditated Domestic Killing

When one spouse kills another for insurance money or other financial gain (also known as a profit murder), or because of threats of divorce or personal disclosures, the suspect will attempt to cover up his act by acting the part of the grieving husband. The suspect will plan the murder and arrange the scene using props and prearranged scenarios to cover up his involvement.

One way this is accomplished is by being a victim himself. He will injure himself to show the police that he attempted to subdue the criminal or protect his loved ones. He will break doors, open windows, ransack the house, place a ski mask and gloves outside on his property just to show that he could not possibly be involved.

Prior to or after the stage is set, the victim will be killed in a way consistent with the scenario. If the story told to police is that the victim fell down a flight of stairs, head injury will be the cause of death. This head injury can be caused by blunt force trauma to the head with an object like a baseball bat—we're sure you get the picture.

Poisoning is usually the preferred method of a very intelligent person who understands the complex procedures needed to cover up this act. On the other hand, a very dumb person, not knowing of the toxicology examination performed at an autopsy, may feel that this is the best way to commit his crime.

Another scenario may be that the spouse places a sedative of some type into a beverage or a dish at dinner. Once the victim passes out, he will be pushed down a flight of stairs or even placed into a vehicle and an accident will be staged. In rural areas, the victim may be put in a situation where the death seems to be caused by animal behavior, such as a kick to the head by a horse.

Adjunct Homicide

When a detective is looking at a homicide, he must take into account the whole scene. He cannot zoom in on just the body; he must look at the complete picture.

Take for example, a burglar surprised by the victim during the course of burglarizing his home. Prior to killing the homeowner, the suspect gained entry into the house. He had to enter rooms and look for items of value to steal. He had to locate something to carry his loot out of the house. This is our criminal's M.O. The killing is secondary. By studying the M.O. of the burglary, the homicide detective can also determine the murderer.

The Cover-up Murder

In a perpetrator's mind, they sometimes must kill people to cover up other acts of crime and violence. A juvenile offender robbing a house is discovered by the homeowner as he walks into his bedroom. The victim will be able to positively identify the juvenile to the police. He will use a weapon at hand, or with the increasing tendency to carry handguns, shoot and kill the victim with the hopes of covering up his burglary.

Sex Offenders

A sex offender will sometimes kill at the conclusion of his sexual assault, usually by some form of strangulation. He may even kill as part of his sexual gratification. This is done in many ways during his assault upon the victim. The sex offender may cause additional mutilation after the killing—vampirism, cannibalism and physical probes of the victim are not uncommon. Souvenirs are sometimes taken, including photographs, videotapes or articles of clothing. Multiple stab wounds and bite marks around the breasts and genitalia are also common.

This type of behavior is the signature aspect of a crime. These criminals will repeat a certain behavior at each crime scene. By acting out their personal fantasies, the killing becomes almost ritualistic as the crimes continue. However, as time goes on, these signatures may expand to more gruesome mutilations postmortem.

When dealing with sadistic or ritualistic criminals, it is important to consider their psychological behavior. The ritualistic or sadistic killer performs to satisfy his mental needs. One of these needs may be to strike fear into the general public, and he wants the world to know that he is the one committing these terrible crimes. To stimulate his own personal fantasies and achieve notoriety, he will incorporate a signature into the killings.

Serial Killers

It is not uncommon for multiple or serial killers to leave a taunting bit of evidence for the police, usually referred to as a calling card. These calling cards are intended to direct police to the suspect or to new victims.

Very violent homicides can be brought on by sexual fantasies manifested by the killer. These fantasies become uncontrollable, causing the suspect to act out his fantasies, slowly at first, but eventually with a growing frenzy. Sexual abuse may occur pre- or postmortem. Serial killers often attack only a particular type of person. His fantasies dictate the victim including hair color and/or length, facial features, body type, age, nationality, or a resemblance to someone from his past.

Sexual assault plays only one part in the modus operandi of serial killers. Some kill because they enjoy the victim's fear and the act of killing. On occasion, serial killers kill the victim in front of family members to gain a sense of domination.

To gain control over victims, a serial killer will use a

number of different methods. He may coax a prostitute into his vehicle on the premise of using her services. He may coax a victim into his vehicle by asking directions or offering a ride. He may even ask for assistance in repairing his vehicle or locating a lost animal.

Once inside the vehicle, control is the first objective. This is done through physical force and/or possession of a weapon. When young people are the victims, verbal threats are used. Another method is to say that they won't be harmed but will be used for a particular situation, such as to gain entry into a building.

These types of homicides usually are performed on victims who are social outcasts. The victims are not involved with family members and are likely to not be reported as missing. Secondly, the criminal wrongly believes when they are reported missing, because they are social outcasts, police will not pursue the case as efficiently.

The victim allows himself to become a victim by being in situations and locations where few people will observe an abduction. One example is a prostitute who stands on street corners in undesirable areas and has no problems with getting into a stranger's vehicle.

Some homicide scenes will be left in such a way that it is shocking or disturbing when they are discovered. Other killers will insert spoons or pieces of wood in the victim's genitals. This is done mainly for curiosity's sake and usually points to a younger male with little or no sexual experience. Mutilation of the victim's genitals usually points to a sexual sadist.

The suspects will, during the course of the crime, have the victim perform certain functions in an attempt to hinder detection by destroying evidence. The victim may be made to shower or wash up after sexual acts. The victim may also be made to clean up areas where the suspect feels evidence might be obtained.

When suspects know the victim prior to killing them, it is not uncommon for the suspect to actively assist the police in an attempt to steer them away from the crime. They will even comfort family members and render assistance to them. This behavior is overly cooperative but can be very distracting to the investigators.

Contract Killing

Contract killings are used by gangs—organized or otherwise—to rid themselves of a member who is perceived as disloyal, a screw-up, or a danger to the gang. La Cosa Nostra, the most notorious organized crime gang of the twentieth century, will usually hire an outsider. They often choose Irish mobsters known as The Westies, because they live predominately on the west side of New York City, and who are calculated, cold-blooded killers who will kill at any time and any place. Their weapon of choice and usual killing method is a shot from a small caliber handgun to the head.

Other contract killings are done by outlaw biker gangs called the 1 percenters. The 1 percenters were given this name in a speech by the president of the American Motorcycle Association. In this speech he stated only 1 percent of all motorcyclists in the United States belong to outlaw biker gangs. The 1 percenters biker colors include the club's emblem, gang name, chapter number and/or chapter location.

Organized crime members like to use the 1 percenters and the Westies because of their vicious nature and their loyalties. They will not divulge to law enforcement the circumstances involved. These contract killings can be as simple as placing an explosive device under the front seat of the target's vehicle. This device is activated when the car is started or by a remote-control device. Other hits could be in the workplace, a sidewalk, a restaurant or any other place where one can easily kill the target.

An assassination could take place as follows: The target is driven to a remote location under the pretense of performing a task. While the target is occupied, a gunman will come up from behind and shoot him at close range in the head. The victim is left where he is shot. Assassins do not want to be apprehended with a body in the trunk of their vehicle. The weapons used are dumped, preferably into a river, making it very difficult, if not impossible, to recover them.

Inner-city gangs generally deal with problem members or members of other gangs themselves. Everyone has heard of drive-by shootings. This is the usual assassination method of ethnic gangs. A plan is formulated and a location, almost always on the opposing gangbanger's turf is picked. Sometimes, a car will be stolen and other times they will use their own vehicle. The vehicle is loaded with four or five gangbangers who drive to the location with the passenger's side facing their target. Upon arrival, they indiscriminately open fire.

Gangbangers prefer high-capacity, large-caliber weapons of mass destruction. They want to spray as many bullets as possible in the shortest time possible. They will use both semiautomatic and fully automatic weapons. AK-47s and 9mm or .45 caliber semiautomatic pistols are most often used. Some of the flashier gangbangers choose chrome-plated weapons. Gangbangers have even been known to possess military hand grenades.

Ritualistic Cults

During the 1960s and early 1970s, Satanism was popular. Satanists believe that the more they kill, the more power they will achieve in hell. The more innocent their victims, the more power they will receive. Thus, babies and virgins are in demand. People are attracted to Satanism because they are attempting to receive the power of demons and use it for themselves. Satanism is growing again and the crimes related to it are increasing, but there is no statistical way to measure the threat. When criminals are arrested, they are arrested for the crime, not for what they believe in.

In teen occult practices, you may or may not find symbols and instruments related to Satanism. In some satanic circles, where sacrificing is performed, ritualistic symbols and other paraphernalia will abound.

A noteworthy case of satanic killing is the night stalker Richard Ramioez who was accused of killing fourteen people. The satanic ritual aspect of the case came out when pentagrams were found at several of the homicide scenes and when a witness testified that she was forced to swear to Satan that she would not call for help when Ramioez left from the scene.

Stabbing

Stabbing deaths account for a large number of homicide-related deaths yearly. Some statistics report that the number of deaths caused by stabbing is just below the number caused by gunshot wounds.

There are two types of injuries caused by sharp items. The first is the stab wound: A pointed object, such as a knife, is pushed through the skin causing injury to the victim. Little or no bruising is observed around the wound. The hilt of some knives may cause bruising. The bleeding associated with the stab wound is internal and little blood is observed at the crime scene. The injuries suffered are internal and to the different organs of the body.

The second is the cut wound: A sharp knife, or other object such as a razor blade, is dragged across the skin causing cuts to the surface of the skin. These injuries will bleed profusely and will only be as deep as the pressure that is applied. Therefore, the injury indicates the amount of force used to make the cut.

Cut wounds are closely related to defense wounds. Defense wounds are injuries suffered by the victim in an attempt to protect himself from the attack. Defense wounds are found on the palms of his hands and on his fingers from when our victim made an attempt to grab the knife. Fingers will be cut deeply causing a large amount of bleeding. When the knife is grabbed by the victim, the perpetrator will pull back with extreme force causing large wounds.

Defense wounds may also be located on the forearms, below the knees on the legs, and sometimes the feet as the victim kicks the assailant.

For suicides, stab and cut wounds are quite different. The victim will show signs of past attempts of suicide: old scars or semi-healed wounds from prior attempts. At the time of the suicide, a number of superficial wounds will be present. These wounds are referred to as *hesitation wounds* and are caused by the victim's attempts to cut himself.

Most suicide lacerations are horizontal. Even with self-inflicted stab wounds, the victim will have hesitation wounds from experimenting prior to the actual suicide. This is one of the ways of determining if a victim was killed by his own hands or those of another.

Some weapons used in stabbings are axes, scissors, forks, screwdrivers, razors, kitchen knives or ice picks. The following cases give an indication of how stab wounds and their attendent (or non-attendent) blood splatter and pooling assist the forensic detective in determing the method of death:

Example 1: A young couple are at home and are complaining about the lack of money to pay their bills. The argument starts in the living room, and proceeds to the bedroom where the wife attempts to take refuge. The husband forces his way into the bedroom by pushing the locked door open. The wife, fearing for her safety, picks up her knitting needles and strikes the husband until he is mortally wounded. The victim's body may show defense wounds on the hands and forearms. The body may also show signs of one or more stab wounds. All injuries to the victim will be pre-mortem. The blood splatter found at the scene will be consistent with the suspect's story and the blood will be contained in one room.

Example 2: Let's take our same young couple and add some complicating factors. The wife wants to leave the husband because she found a better lover, but she knows that if she gets a divorce, she will walk away with little or no money. The wife and boyfriend plan to kill the husband and to make the homicide appear to be self defense. In this case, the husband may be found in the kitchen area or the bedroom. The husband will show few or no defense wounds because the attack will be a surprise. The stab wounds will be numerous and may even be found on his back. Some stab wounds will be postmortem.

The victim's body will contain both cut and stab wounds and the blood splatter will not be consistent with the suspect's story. The blood splatter will be consistent with defensive behavior such as fleeing from room to room and there will be blood pooling where the victim has stopped to defend himself.

Example 3: A middle-aged fellow is walking home from work and, prior to arriving home, he is stopped and robbed by the neighborhood gang at knife point. Our victim, having been robbed numerous times in the past, decides he is going to fight back. The victim is found the next morning with a single stab wound to the chest. Little or no blood will be observed at the scene. Most of the victim's bleeding will be internal, leaving small blood staining around the wound on the victim's clothing.

Example 4: A young woman is walking to her vehicle after leaving work one night. The suspect grabs her from behind, places a large knife to her throat, and demands that she obey his requests. The victim is then taken to a waiting van where she is forced to lie on her stomach while her hands are secured behind her with duct tape. The victim's eyes and mouth are also covered with duct tape to prevent her from calling for assistance and seeing the suspect. The victim's body will show bruises caused by rough treatment at the hands of the suspect. The victim will show signs of sexual assault and will receive from one to multiple stab wounds depending on the psychological motivation of her attacker.

Death by Gunshot

Before we get into some examples, let's take a moment to discuss the different types of weapons and wounds that one will find. The so-called small arms are basically weapons that can be carried easily and comfortably by one person. They include machine guns, submachine guns, handguns, shotguns and rifles. We have, on occasion, observed cases involving cross bows and long bows. In most cases involving a bow and arrow, the person using these weapons has a hunting background, and these weapons are readily at hand.

Handguns come in many forms from the very simple to the very complex. Zip guns are homemade single shot pistols usually carried by gang members and guerrilla fighters. Only one round of ammunition can be inserted and fired.

Derringers and Saturday Night Specials are small, cheaply-made handguns. Most Derringers contain chambers for two rounds and can only be fired one at a time. The Saturday Night Specials are knock offs of more expensive revolvers.

Revolvers, or wheel guns, are pistols with a two- to twelve-inch barrel. The rounds are inserted into the wheeled chamber, which can hold from five to eight rounds. The shell casings will remain inside the chamber until they are physically ejected.

The auto-loading pistols, which are also called semi-automatic handguns, use a magazine to contain the rounds. The magazine is placed into the pistol grip, and shells are fed into the cylinder by the action of the slide. After firing, the shell casing is ejected from the weapon.

For those of you who are unfamiliar with the make up of a round, it contains four components:

1. Bullet
2. Shell casing
3. Powder
4. Primer.

The bullet, or projectile, is the portion that leaves the barrel of the weapon. The shell casing holds the powder, a flammable propellant similar to black powder, and the bullet. The final component is the primer, which rests at the base of the round. When struck by the weapon's firing pin, it creates an ignition source for the powder, which ignites and turns into gases that force the bullet out of the shell casing and down the barrel of the weapon.

The basic sizes of ammunition used for semi-automatic handguns are (starting from the smallest): .22 caliber, .25 caliber, .32 caliber, .380 caliber, 9mm, .40 caliber, 10mm and .45 caliber. Other handgun calibers used primarily for revolvers are: .38 caliber, .357 caliber, .41 caliber and .44 caliber. Caliber refers to the diameter of the muzzle, or opening, of a gun's barrel and is measured either in hundredths or thousandths of an inch or in millimeters.

Handguns are popular weapons because they are easy to conceal. Because they are so popular, we are going to concentrate on them.

The bullet creates a number of different injuries referred to as gunshot wounds. These wounds are classified into four categories, based on the distance from the muzzle of the weapon to the victim at the time of injury:

1. The *contact wound*, occurs when the muzzle of the gun is placed directly against the victim's body.
2. The *near contact wound* when the muzzle of the gun does not come in physical contact with the victim's body but is only a short distance away (one to three inches).
3. The *intermediate gunshot wound* occurs when the muzzle of the gun is six to eight inches away from the victim but close enough to have the victim burnt by the gunpowder. This burning is also known as *powder tattooing*. Powder tattoos can be found on the clothing or skin of the victim.
4. The *distant wound* occurs when the muzzle of the gun is more than fifteen to eighteen inches from the victim and no injury other than the bullet passing through the skin is apparent.

When investigating gunshot wounds, the official will take into consideration the size or caliber of the weapon. Basically, the smaller the weapon, the closer the weapon needs to be for powder tattooing. When examining the body, the official will also look for the direction or path of the bullet. This is determined through a number of observations and can give clues to the type of killing. For instance, a person usually does not commit suicide by holding a gun to the back of his own head.

The entrance wound is where the bullet enters and is identified by powder tattooing, if the weapon is close enough, and/or the abrasion wound, which happens when the bullet passes through the skin. The rotating action of the bullet causes the skin around it to abrade where the bullet enters. This abrasion appears as a reddish mark around the hole itself. Entrance wounds are usually small, the size of the projectile including the abrasive ring.

Exit wounds, no matter the distance from which the weapon is fired, are larger, more irregular and usually do not have the abrasion ring.

Experts use the aforementioned characteristics to determine the path of the bullet and the distance of the weapon from the victim. This is extremely helpful in verifying the suspect's account of what happened.

When dealing with homicides that occur indoors, it is important to remember that, whether it be a domestic dispute or a sexual sadist, most of the bullets will hit the mark. This is mainly because of the close proximity of the weapon to the victim.

Things to Remember

Most criminals are apprehended because they don't realize the clues they leave behind. This is especially true of homicides. Even the most carefully laid plan can result in an arrest. Here are a few ways the manner of death can lead to an arrest.

Strangulation. Here's an example of killing someone for greed, an important motivation. One scenario is the business partnership where one partner wants to buy out the other partner and is unsuccessful. The business contract indicates that upon death, the surviving associate will maintain controlling interest. Our greedy partner decides that he will kill his partner to obtain control.

He has decided that the best way is to have the victim

appear to hang himself and sets his plan into action. He will speak with employees and other associates about how he feels that his partner is down in the dumps lately to plant the idea of suicide among co-workers.

After work one night he uses the associate's personal typewriter to type a heart-felt suicide note and then signs the note by tracing the signature. The day of the killing, he will ask the victim to stay a little later to go over some business details. When the office is empty, the killer will make his way behind the victim and using a piece of clothesline, which he retrieved from his garage earlier that day, strangle the victim.

Now, you are all thinking that the victim sees the rope and starts to fight back. What we must remember here is that the victim has no idea of what is happening. He feels entirely comfortable with his partner. The killer has no need to wear gloves because his fingerprints would normally be found throughout the office. Once the victim has succumbed to the attack, the clothesline is removed and the victim is moved to a coat rack and the clothesline is replaced with the victim's telephone cord. The rope is taken from the scene by the assailant and prior to leaving, the suicide note is placed in an obvious location on the victim's desk.

The next day the killer will be late for work so that someone else finds the body. Now, remember, he told co-workers and friends of his partner's depression and placed the suicide note in an obvious location. The police respond and observe the suicide note and the lack of any signs of struggle in the office. There's only one problem, our killer left a handful of clues. The victim's secretary knows that the victim worked late with his partner. The victim's wife is aware of the attempted takeover of the company. The victim's body shows the rope imprint. Through handwriting analysis, it is determined that the signature was indeed forged by tracing.

Accidents That Aren't. A husband returns home and finds his wife lying face down in a water-filled bathtub. Apparently, a slip and fall resulted in accidental drowning. The police arrive and examine the scene and observe no signs of foul play in the residence especially in the bathroom area. The scene is documented and the victim removed.

The next day, an autopsy is performed, and the victim's body is carefully examined. Close examination of the victim's neck reveal injuries from abrasions and lacerations. These injuries were not visible until the victim's body was thoroughly dry.

The lacerations are from the fingernails of the killer as he strangled her and the victim's own fingernails as she attempted to free herself. The other abrasions are from the killer's hands squeezing the life from her. During the autopsy, we found that the tissue on her neck contained hemorrhages. The victim's larynx was fractured and we found an additional fracture in the thyroid and the cricoid cartilages. The hyoid bone was also fractured, indicating signs of strangulation.

When examining the injury to the head, which at first appeared to be from slipping on the slick surface of the tub, an autopsy revealed quite a different scenario. The injury was to the top of the victim's head. The hemorrhages were linear and caused by an impact with a hard rounded object consistent with a small piece of metal pipe found in the garage. Upon examination in the laboratory, the pipe showed blood stains.

Decomposition. Decomposing victims can help an investigation in some ways and severely hinder it in others. The rate of decomposition helps detectives determine the time of death. The medical examiner must take into consideration the temperature and condition of the body. If the victim is placed in a refrigerated box, the rate of decomposition will be quite slow. Think of it as chicken stored in your refrigerator versus chicken stored in the freezer. Which will last longer?

Another factor in decomposing is the effects that animal and insects have. Animals eat the flesh, which increases the decomposing.

When examining a severely decomposed body, it is

hard to determine any soft tissue damage caused by sharp or blunt objects. The skeleton will show broken bones and bones that were cut by stab wounds. Animal activity and gravity will separate bullets from the victim over time. Careful excavation is necessary when dealing with decomposed bodies and skeletons.

Mutilation. In passion killings, the injury to the victim is done out of rage and will continue until the weapon is spent or the rage subsides. Psychotic mutilations can be surgically precise and sexual in nature, e.g., the removal of the nipples. In sadistic killings, mutilation will be to terrorize and cause pain by slashing the victim with a knife or assaulting the victim with fist or other implements like metal pipes.

In sexually sadistic killings, ropes or cords will be used and placed around the breasts, neck and hands, not only to secure the victim but also for the sexual pleasure of the perpetrator. Elaborate, erotic gags and blindfolds may also be used.

Suicide or Homicide

Let's see how good all you supersleuths really are! Or, are you reading the last chapter first? What we are going to do now is give you a real-life scenario so that all you Dick Tracy's out there can solve the crime.

Suzy Sweetheart is an attractive woman in her late thirties. Suzy has dated frequently, but never married. It has been said that Suzy dresses a little bit too sexy for her own good. Suzy lives in an apartment building a few blocks from her job.

A co-worker becomes alarmed at the fact that Suzy, who has never taken a sick day, has not reported to work and failed to call in. She contacts the police and reports her fear. The police dispatch a patrol car to Suzy's apartment.

The patrol officer knocks on Suzy's door and receives no response. The officer then knocks at the next apartment and is informed by the neighbor that Suzy was last seen returning from work the previous evening. The officer then attempts to locate Suzy by again knocking on her door. The officer, upon receiving no response, turns the door knob and finds it to be locked.

The officer summons the superintendent and requests that the door be opened. Once the door is opened, the officer locates the victim on the floor of her bedroom, bound with rope. At this time, the officer secures the scene and summons the Major Crime and Forensic Units. The Forensic Unit responds and after properly documenting the scene, a cursory examination is conducted.

The victim is lying on her bedroom floor at the foot of the bed. She is face down and completely naked. Her legs are bent at the knee and her feet are resting against her buttocks. Both feet are secured with rope and another rope connects them to a loop of rope around her neck. Also around her neck, under the rope is a very expensive silk scarf. The victim's hands are bound loosely behind her back just above her buttocks. Under the victim's body is a sheet from the bed, which appears to have been placed there in an attempt to cover or carry the victim from the scene.

Nothing else is out of place and no signs of a struggle are observed. The only other item is that a patio door leading from her bedroom is unlocked and slightly ajar.

The Major Crime detectives canvasing the area have located two neighbors, one living across the hall and one in the apartment next to the victim, who report that in the past they have overheard the victim arguing violently with her boyfriend. Upon interviewing the boyfriend, he admits to having had arguments with the victim, but states that he never hit her and the last time he spoke with her was over the phone at her job the day before she was found.

The victim's cause of death was determined at the autopsy to be asphyxiation. No other injuries were observed on any location of the victim's body. Livor Mortis is consistent with the position of the body after death. No signs of sexual assault were found. OK, now, go bring the suspect in for processing. So, what do you think? Definitely a homicide, probably by the boyfriend? Well, if you want to find out, you have to purchase our next book!

E I G H T

KIDNAPPING

Kidnapping occurs when a person removes or unlawfully confines another person for the purpose of a shield, hostage, reward or ransom. Kidnapping is one of the most terrifying and cruel crimes that can be committed against another human being. In our opinion, kidnapping has more impact than homicide because of the uncertainty of the victim's whereabouts, condition and the likelihood of being reunited with the victim. It is difficult for the family to move on while these uncertainties weigh upon them.

Gang Kidnappings

Organized Crime

Organized crime has used kidnapping throughout the years to gain control over rival gangs and government officials. Key personnel or their family members are kidnapped and used as negotiating pawns.

Their goal is to complete the kidnapping with little or no outside interference. The kidnap target will be followed by one or perhaps two vehicles. When the kidnappers believe it is safe, they block the target's vehicle to prevent escape. Once the victim's vehicle is stopped, he is forcibly transferred to the kidnapper's vehicle.

The victim is then secured with handcuffs or other binding. If the victim is struggling, his feet will be secured too. Sometimes mace or another chemical agent is sprayed in his face to debilitate him. Eventually, the victim will be blindfolded and gagged with a piece of cloth or duct tape. His eyes will be covered with duct tape, cloth or perhaps a hood.

The kidnapper's vehicle is usually stolen to prevent any chance of tracing the vehicle. Following successful completion of the kidnapping, the vehicle may be set ablaze to conceal any evidence that may have been left in it. In some cases, the kidnappers will use their own vehicles. But, if they feel that they were observed during the kidnapping, they will drive the vehicle to a remote location and report it stolen. The victim is driven to a safehouse, maybe the basement of a gang member's house, where chances of being discovered are minimal.

Money is only one type of ransom. In organized crime kidnappings, the ransom is often control over a situation such as not giving testimony, signing over property or control of a business, and agreeing to do their bidding, which may include buying or shipping products from the kidnappers. If the demands are met, the victim will be returned to his family. If not, there is a good possibility that he will end up dead.

Ransom demands could be made through a number of different routes. It could be as simple as using a pay phone to call a newspaper or the victim's family and make the demands. When using a pay phone, it is a good idea to use a different phone each time a call is made to prevent a trace and subsequent surveillance of the area. Other methods of delivering demands are by U.S. mail using hand-written letters from the victim or the notorious letters made of words cut from newspapers or magazines. In some circumstances, a typewriter may be used for the letter.

Asian Gangs

Asian gangs perform their kidnappings in a very flamboyant way because their main purpose is to terrorize their victims. A common scenario: The gang enters a restaurant where the victim's family is having dinner, and at gun point removes the victim from the premises. Or, they kidnap a family member at home as he arrives from work. Family members are often assaulted and, if enough resistance is given, a family member may even be shot. The victim will be bound and gagged with rope, duct tape or handcuffs, placed into the rear of a van or the trunk of a vehicle and transported to an apartment or warehouse.

The ransom demands will be given at the scene and little or no communication will occur between the kidnappers and the victim's family. Once the demands are met, the victim may or may not be released to his family. Ransom will most likely be for control over a business, for protection money, money laundering or to silence a witness.

Another method may be to have a family member who is still living in their country of origin receive threats of death or incarceration if the family members in the United States do not cooperate.

Drug Lords

Leaders of narcotic trafficking gangs find kidnapping a useful tool in conducting business. They target judges to throw a monkeywrench into prosecution efforts or political leaders to suppress additional laws against narcotic trafficking. Narcotic traffickers usually do not seek money because they make substantial money from their narcotics trafficking. When a government official refuses a bribe, the drug lords attempt to gain control over them by kidnapping. When all efforts fail, they are generally murdered.

Drug lords differ from other organized crime leaders because they have extraordinary power over their communities. This power comes from supplying employment and other basic needs for their communities especially in developing countries. These needs can include education, medical care, housing and transportation. This power not only protects the drug lords, but assists them in hiding their victims.

The drug lord will assign members of his organization to kidnap a victim at his residence. The victim could be a family member or the official himself. Once in control of the victim, the demands will be given to him and he will be released. The victim knows that the drug lords mean business, and since they kidnapped him once, they can easily do it again.

Ransom Seekers

The ransom seeker chooses his target for the express purpose of making money. Surveillance is conducted and a plan is formulated, including methods of restraint and transportation, time and location of the kidnapping. The time and location are picked to minimize the possibility of outside interference. A location, which has no connection to the kidnappers, is picked to house the victim. The kidnappers use disguises or masks to cover their faces, wear gloves, and travel in stolen vehicles.

Once the kidnapping is performed, the victim will remain at one location, and the kidnappers make their ransom demands either through the mail or at various pay telephones. If it is through the mail, the correspondence may be cut and pasted, typewritten or handwritten. Delivery instructions are given once the kidnappers know the victim's family will pay the ransom. No matter how much pre-planning was involved, someone physically has to pick up the money and return to a location, making apprehension almost certain. Kidnappers, in an attempt to elude apprehension, will demand that the pick-up man return safely before the victim is released. The pick-up man will not return to where the victim is located, but instead will travel to a location where he feels that no one has followed him.

In some cases, victims, instead of being returned to

their families, are found dead. This is because of an unexpected event like a medical condition or an escape attempt which fatally injures the victim. From time to time poor directions to the victim's location cause a delay in finding him, and the victim dies from exposure or the binding the kidnapper used to restrain him.

Once a person is kidnapped and the ransom demand is made, a charge of extortion can also be levied against the kidnapper. Extortion is the threat of harm for the purpose of obtaining property (in this case, a person's money).

Cults

Fanatic religious cults kidnap by seeking out potential members. These victims come from all walks of life, but they all have a desire to belong. Cult members slowly seduce their victims with promises of happiness and spiritual fulfillment. This procedure is time-consuming and is carried out over an extended period of time. Eventually, victims are asked to attend a series of lectures or meetings where the brainwashing begins. These meetings are choreographed in such a way that the leader appears to be a deity, apostle or disciple of God. Cult members appear affectionate during these meetings, but behave so the victim feels intimidation and a need to participate. This is usually done by telling the victim of all the good and miracles performed by the spiritual leader.

The brainwashing usually starts off with an overload of information designed to cause confusion and a belief that friends and family are outsiders and are attempting to, in some way, harm or prevent the spiritual transformation the victim is seeking. This is often performed by sleep deprivation. Upon entering a cult, meetings and worship will continue for days. The cultists will not actually say that you cannot sleep, but they will tell the victim that to achieve enlightenment, he must continue to worship no matter how tired he feels. Depriving the victim of water, food and bathroom facilities re-enforces the brainwashing. The cultists do this by explaining that the ability to control one's basic needs is the first step to controlling one's thoughts.

The victim will not be given a chance to act on their

own without constant supervision, until the cult feels it is safe to give the victim some freedom. The victim is informed that to become a true member, he must release all outside financial bonds, properties and money to the organization. All of the victim's finances are eventually turned over to the group and all outside contact with family members ceases.

The group suppresses all efforts by family members and law enforcement authorities to personally contact the victim. The victim may be moved around from state to state. All financial and basic needs are provided by the cult so the victim is dependant on the group for mere survival.

When Mauro worked as a detective sergeant for a police department, he was responsible for fingerprinting and performing background checks on all people entering the town for solicitation purposes. This was done by order of the township for the protection of the citizens of the community.

One summer Saturday morning, a group of around twenty-five members of a well-known religious cult was reported soliciting and selling poor-quality silk flowers. The patrols located the supervisor of the group who was ordered to report with all members to police headquarters for processing.

The permits cost five dollars each, which was paid by the group leader, and the only identification the other group members had was a picture ID issued by the cult. While filling out the permit application, Mauro discovered they were from all over the world—Australia, South Africa, Europe and Asia.

When dealing with religious cults, one must realize that the leaders have a great deal of control over their victims. This was proven by Jim Jones and the People's Temple; Jones ordered all 912 of his followers to commit suicide rather than return to the United States.

Fanatics and Terrorists

Fanatics and terrorists use kidnapping in an attempt to gain publicity for their cause. They will also use it to frighten people and to achieve financial gains. These people are the most dangerous because they truly believe in their cause and feel that what they are doing is right.

Mauro interviewed a former member of a well-known terrorist group who was in prison. When Mauro asked him how he got involved, he stated that he truly believed that his group was going to overthrow the United States government, and he, along with other members, would do anything to accomplish this goal.

He was incarcerated for his involvement in robbing armored cars. The money obtained by robbing these vehicles was used to supply items the group needed to survive. These items included safehouses in different areas of the country, transportation, basic living staples, as well as weapons and explosives.

While questioning him further, Mauro asked him how he would overthrow not only the law enforcement community, but the military and the common people of our nation. He replied that his group was strong enough to start the revolution and that once it was started, the nation would join their cause. He also stated that he felt like a colonialist during the Revolutionary War, and that he would be responsible for overthrowing the U.S. government, just as his forefathers declared their independence from England.

These types of groups will normally make a dramatic kidnapping to increase their publicity. They wear military clothes and carry military weapons. We all remember the kidnapping and eventual enlistment of Patty Hearst in the Symbionese Liberation Army. Once kidnapped, she was brainwashed through isolation; she was left alone for days at a time locked in a closet. She was told when to eat, when to shower, when to use the bathroom, and all this time, she was blindfolded and tied up by her captors.

Political propaganda was recited to her over and over, and she was told that her lifestyle and that of her family was unjust. Eventually, all this physical abuse and mental anguish took its toll and she began to accept the teachings of her captors. She was so involved with the organization at one point that she participated in violent criminal activity.

A terrorist will never avoid a conflict and will be willing to sacrifice their comrades or themselves for their cause. Their victims will probably be sacrificed or be turned into a group member if held long enough.

Terrorist kidnappings are well planned and carried out with military precision. A plan will be formulated taking advantage of weak security precautions. This may occur when the target is dropping off his child for piano lessons or when he is rendezvousing with a mistress.

As our victim reaches the location of the kidnapping, the passenger of a motorcycle fires a handgun at the driver or tires to stop the vehicle. Once the vehicle is stopped, the kidnappers jump out and break the vehicle's windshield with a baseball bat or large stone. A car or van will arrive to transport the victim away from the scene quickly. The victim is secured with handcuffs or duct tape placed around his hands, feet and mouth. The victim will be placed into a trunk of a car or in the rear of a van.

The kidnappers will then drive to a location where the victim will be kept. The victim will probably be moved periodically from place to place to avoid detection. The ransom demands will be sent in a note by courier or in a videotaped message showing the victim to assure the authorities that they indeed have him. Sometimes, ransom arrangements will be made via the telephone or through a television, radio station or local newspaper.

Terrorists usually demand ransom to carry on "the cause." This ransom will include large amounts of money, sometimes in the millions, and of course the release of political comrades who are incarcerated around the world. These ransom demands are basically made for the benefit of the media rather than for the monetary gain. Think back to the kidnappings and hijackings which happened in Iran and Beirut; money became secondary to coverage of the cause.

In some cases, to assure the authorities that their demands must be met, the victim will have a body part removed and shipped to the family.

Did you ever wonder why no Communist officials or citizens were ever kidnapped? This is because once a high-ranking official of the KGB was kidnapped in a Mideast country. An investigation was conducted and one of the kidnappers was kidnapped and cut into little bitty pieces, leaving only his head intact. By the way, they used a chain saw to do this. After the dismemberment, the KGB carefully wrapped his body parts in a box, so the victim's face stared up at the kidnappers when the box was opened. The victim's body was accompanied by a short note describing what would happen to the remainder of the group if the kidnap victim was not returned. This merry package was dropped off in front of the leader's residence. Needless to say, within twenty-four hours, the kidnap victim was returned safely.

Parental Abduction

When a spouse is divorcing, it is usually over strong conflict or physical abuse. One spouse may be intent on leaving the other for another love interest. There may be sexual abuse or domestic violence directed toward the children. Sometimes the noncustodial parent abducts the child or children in the family.

If the abducting noncustodial parent feels that she is doing this to protect her children from additional sexual abuse, she may remove the children by telling them that they are going for a ride. This is the beginning of the abduction. The parent tells the children that their other parent does not love them anymore, or she will fabricate other stories in an attempt to distance the children from the rest of the family.

In the United States today, underground movements assist noncustodial parents in eluding law enforcement, getting custody returned to them, and providing basic life support. These underground movements are made up of families and sympathetic supporters of abused and neglected children. They set aside basements and other areas in their homes to accommodate the runners. They will provide them with food, transportation, money and legal expenses to assist them in their time of need. When a location gets discovered or after a certain amount of time, the family is moved to another location, which could be in the same town or several states away. This underground movement contacts sympathetic family members by mailing letters to an out-of-state safehouse who in turn will either forward the letters to another location or deliver them to the family.

Parents who are not citizens of the United States will abduct their child and return to their home country. Sometimes the noncustodial parent arranges a vacation to his native country on the premise of meeting family members. Once they arrive or a short time later, the custodial parent will be informed that the children are not returning to the United States. There is nothing the spouse can do to have the child returned to the United States, other than kidnapping the child in return.

Stranger Abduction

It is not really known nor could it be precisely analyzed what percentage of abductions are by a stranger. Because of the runaway population, throwaway kids or family members involved in the disappearance of their children, an exact figure can not be determined.

When a stranger abduction occurs, it is usually a random event and the child does not have the ability to escape or seek help. The offender could be a drifter, which makes it incredibly hard to locate or even to identify him. When stranger abduction occurs, they will be driving their own vehicles and lure the child over to the vehicle with promise of a reward, a plea for assistance, or by stating that they are there on behalf of their parents, who have been injured, and they need the child's assistance. Once in the vehicle, the abductor will secure the victim with physical restraints and make a quick getaway. The offender makes the abduction for a variety of reasons. There may be a sexual connection where the offender will seek out a certain sex, age and type of victim, known as a *profile*.

Some offenders maintain custody for just a short time, where others keep the child until they become a liability or no longer fit their sexual profile. Offenders may trade their victims to each other or eventually kill them and dispose of them in an isolated area, out of state, so when they are found, identification is nearly impossible. Stranger abduction is considered by some to be performed by a network of offenders, where victims are taken and passed around and abused throughout the United States. Others believe that there is no network and that only a few offenders are responsible for the abductions committed in the United States.

Serial Killer as Kidnapper

When you have offenders who abduct children or adults for the purpose of killing them, called serial killers, we classify them as kidnappers. Most serial killers prefer a certain type of victim, often a person who will not be readily missed. Prostitutes and the homeless are ideal victims. Most prostitutes are loners and have no real contact with family members or loved ones on a regular basis. Quick notification of the absence of these victims is uncommon.

Most serial killers follow a pattern because they are comfortable with it. They figure if it worked once, it will surely work again. The abductor will select a certain type of victim and will stay within that range. This range includes age, hair color, body type and area of abduction along with area of disposal, which will be a remote, desolate area. The abductor lures the victim into his vehicle and once inside, he will overpower and secure the victim. He may use duct tape, rope or hand cuffs and will also have some type of weapon on him. He may first sexually abuse the victim, then slowly torture, and finally kill. Some will kill their victims just for the pleasure of killing.

Apprehending Kidnappers

The chances of apprehension of a kidnapper seeking a reward, especially in the United States, is great. The apprehension will be made through the many contacts the kidnappers have to make to secure the delivery of their reward or when they attempt to retrieve the ransom. The arrest comes either at the location of the drop off to the kidnappers or the ransom carrier will be followed through surveillance, back to where the victim is located.

Kidnappers as ransom seekers, other than the Asian gangs, do not generally think through the consequences of their actions. In past kidnappings, almost all kidnappers were apprehended.

NINE

PROSTITUTION

Prostitution has been defined by the law as the practice of offering your body indiscriminately for money or its equivalent. The President's Commission on Law Enforcement reports that there were over 50,000 arrests for prostitution and commercialized vice in 1985. In 1992, the figures were 76,400 arrests nationwide, which assumes that approximately 65,000 persons were engaged in such activity with a total yearly income of $322 million. Other studies have claimed that prostitution involves 100,000 to 500,000 men and women in the United States and that the profession itself grosses more than a billion dollars a year.

It is a simple fact of life that some people either prefer to or have to pay for sex, and as long as there are people willing to pay for it, there will be others willing to sell it. It is a classic case of supply and demand, just like any business.

Citizens complain that prostitution makes it impossible to carry on legitimate businesses in some parts of the cities. New Yorkers lament that prostitutes have caused a deterioration of Times Square; Hollywood merchants claim their area has become known as a hookers' paradise; officials everywhere point an accusing finger at court decisions that they say have made it almost impossible to control prostitution effectively. Boston has attempted to segregate vice areas of the city into red zones, while in Salt Lake City, police have taken to arresting the clients of prostitutes known as *johns*. In other cities cooperating news media publish the names of men picked up for soliciting prostitutes. Periodic vice raids are used to round up prostitutes in many cities, but in spite of these and other efforts, prostitution continues to flourish. Some officials have urged that prostitution be legalized as it is in Germany and other parts of Europe, which means not so much legalization as regulation. In the United States, Nevada has more or less adopted such a plan. But what works in Nevada might not work in other areas of the country, since those areas of the state where prostitution is legalized are very small towns, the inhabitants of which are fewer than those in a block of urban apartment buildings.

Today's brothel is likely to be right around the corner in the form of a massage parlor, a nude photo club, an escort service, dial-a-massage, a sauna house or some other thinly disguised market for sexual services. The motive for the prostitute's client appears to remain much the same: the craving for sexual variety, perverse gratification and intercourse free of entangling commitments. As for the prostitute herself, the evidence suggests that now, as in the past, her activity is voluntary, representing for some a considerable range of advantages including flexible work hours, contact with diverse people of power and influence, a heightened sense of activity, and the opportunity to make substantial sums of money.

A Brief History of Prostitution

In ancient Greece the lowest prostitutes were street walkers and brothel inmates. Far above both were the *hetaerae*, who were distinguished by being educated in the arts and by serving only the wealthy and powerful. They provided entertainment and intellectual companionship, as well as sexual gratification. The *hetaerae*, drawn from the population, compensated for the fact that wives and daughters were not permitted to entertain, go outside the home, or acquire an education. In fact, Demosthenes summed it up when he said, "Man has the *hetaerae* for erotic enjoyments, girlfriends for daily use, and wives to bring up children and to be faithful housewives."

Similarly, Japan until very recently had three classes of women outside of respectable family life: the *joro* in brothels, the *jogoku* or unlicensed prostitutes on the streets or in bath houses, and the *geisha* or dancing girls. Trained in dancing, singing and other methods of entertaining guests in tea houses, geisha girls were an indispensable adjunct to Japanese entertainment. However, not all of them were open to prostitution, and if they were, they were selective in their customers.

In modern society about all that is left of prostitution is the commercial form, in which one party uses sex for pleasure, the other for money. To tie intercourse to sheer pleasure is to divorce it from both reproduction and from any sentimental social relationship. This does not mean that people feel as strongly about prostitution as they do about thieves or arsonists. A recent survey conducted by *McCall's* magazine found that only 7 percent of the respondents said they would clear the streets of prostitutes if they had the chance. The distaste for prostitution is manifested mainly by reluctance to have a bordello in the neighborhood, or to be identified with the business or its personnel. Otherwise, it does not seem to bother the general population.

Causes of Prostitution

If prostitution offends the moral principles of people, why does it exist? And, if it denigrates women, how does it recruit its members? To explain prostitution in economic terms is begging the question. Since prostitution is defined as selling sexual favors, one might say that retail merchandising has economic causes.

Prostitution arises from the demand for the prostitute's services. This need for service arises out of the regulation of sex itself and the limited liability of a commercial sexual relationship. If the customer has money, he can obtain satisfaction with no further obligations. In the case of a female prostitute, the only clients that she needs to procure are men. A john, or client of the prostitute, does not become enmeshed in courtship, friendship or marriage. Let's face it, every male finds himself sometimes, and some males find themselves most of the time, in circumstances where sexual release through more reputable channels is impossible.

Our experiences have shown that, of course, not all males visit prostitutes, but those who do depend on them for a major portion of their sexual activity. About 30 percent of men have never had contact with prostitutes. Of the rest, most have had only one or two experiences. No more than 15 to 20 percent of men visit a prostitute more often than a few times a year. This still leaves a substantial portion of the adult male population. For them, what does prostitution provide that other outlets cannot?

The primary advantage of prostitution for these men is its impartiality, impersonality and economy. Attracting and seducing a woman can be costly. By its effort to contain sexual acts in a meaningful and enduring social relationship, society creates advantages for prostitution. For less than the cost of a single date with a girl who is not a prostitute, a male can engage in whatever sexual fantasies he desires with a prostitute. Additionally, the impersonality of prostitution makes it particularly suited to strangers. The man away from his wife or circle of girlfriends cannot, in a short time, count on seducing a respectable woman. Also, since certain sexual acts are considered immoral for wives and sweethearts, the prostitute has an advantage. That is, the prostitute, as long as she gets paid, will usually perform 99.9 percent of the services requested by the client. The demand for prostitution will not be eliminated or seriously altered by a change in the economic system. The underlying basis for the demand is inherent in human society.

Prostitute Categories

Now it's time to put on our hot pants, lipstick and high-heeled shoes and check out the action on the streets.

The Legalized Brothel

In some countries prostitution is a legal, commercial venture. Brothels are licensed and regulated by the government in an effort to minimize the negative impacts of venereal disease and organized crime. These two side effects of prostitution are generally present in situations where prostitution is illegal.

In Nevada, the practice of legalized brothels is accepted in almost all of the seventeen counties of the state. The Mustang Ranch, one of the fifty or more licensed brothels is the largest, doing an annual business of between $3 and $5 million. The house rules are not too strict. Drugs and sloppy clothes are not allowed. There are between twenty and twenty-five women working in this establishment at any given time. They are regularly inspected by physicians and are required to hang their health certificates on the walls. The average income of the women is approximately $600 to $700 per week, of which $300 goes for room and board. The women are free to accept or reject customers for any reason. They may, for example, discriminate against clients from different ethnic backgrounds. Whether or not the legal brothel has resulted in an increase or decrease in venereal disease or AIDS cannot be established. It has, however, decreased the activity of the police and courts in Nevada in dealing with prostitution.

The Illegal Brothel

In the United States most brothels that operate do so illegally. A common scene in New York City is luxurious east-side apartment houses, catering to New York and visiting businessmen.

Sue, the proprietor of the brothel, receives a minimum

of $700 every few days tax free. A *trick*, which is a sexual act, costs anywhere from $35 to $75 and the money is divided equally with the hooker. Sue calls the hookers or prostitutes to work when they are needed. Sue is perpetually looking for new women to satisfy her customers. She usually hears of women from other hookers.

Sue considers her apartment a clean, respectable place that gentlemanly clientele can frequent. She avoids troublesome or aging hookers. Troublesome hookers are those who give out their home telephone numbers, which Sue considers stealing, and those who don't share the money that they have made from a client.

To prevent detection by the police, Sue pays off the doorman and the building manager, and the owners of the building seem oblivious as long as the rent is paid. Every two or three years, Sue changes her apartment and her telephone number, in the process dropping a few johns, who either showed violent tendencies or didn't pay enough money. However, Sue must always stay on the right side of the clients she drops because they can always go to the police.

The Street Walker

In many respects the street walker is at the bottom of the prostitution hierarchy. The most common scene that we have experienced is a young girl, either a runaway or a throwaway child, who drifts to the big city after leaving her home. She could be running away from sexual abuse by family members or friends. She often works as a waitress or clerk and for a time lives a rootless, disorganized life without friends and without ties to any social institutions. During this crucial period she is dissatisfied, tense, bitter and bewildered. She is far away from home and away from things that, even though they were uncomfortable, were her mainstay in her younger years. Her shiftless, alienated way of life brings her into contact with established prostitutes, who on the surface seem to be very well off and have good job security. Her morals are at a low, and she hungers for some kind of friendship and affection, so she will accept dates arranged for her by a prostitute friend or the prostitute's pimp.

What is a very common sight in New York City is for the pimps to be wandering around the Port Authority Terminal, which is the largest bus terminal in the United States. As these runaway or throwaway children enter the Port Authority, they are overwhelmed by the vastness and are easy to spot as new to the area. The pimps, who are male, frequent the coffee shops and rest areas of the Port Authority and attempt to strike up a conversation with these runaways. They offer them shelter for the night or possibly a part-time job or some money. They want to build up a friendship so that they can have this girl dependent on them. Some of them may actually come right out and request that they work for them as prostitutes. However, most of them state that they would be willing to have these women work as escorts for young men who need affection and attention at social events.

These young women, unaware of city life, enter into these relationships with pimps not knowing that it is really a front for hardcore prostitution. Eventually, the pimp moves from friendship to initiating the girl into prostitution either by raping the girl himself, or having multiple members of his circle of pimps rape her repeatedly until she gets accustomed to rough sex.

The curious relationship between prostitutes and pimps, to whom they turn over a large part of their earnings, is seen as an attempt by the women to overcome loneliness and form a relationship with someone who seems to be lower than themselves.

Once the girl is degraded into this type of life, she becomes the pimp's servant and works for him where and when he tells her to. In return for these services, the pimp will give the girl free room and board, and, of course, she must have sex with him or any of his friends whenever they desire. Eventually, some street walkers will move from one pimp to another. However, if she moves, it will be a tremendous distance away from the original pimp, as pimps have certain territories and zones. The girl is only supplied with free room and board as long as she works for the pimp. Should she decide to go out on her own, she must work even harder to make money to have a place to stay. Some women who successfully do go on their own and escape from the pimps will arrange to live with other hookers so that they can share the rent.

Eventually, street walkers will move outside lawful society when they get arrested. After a time, the arrest experience is viewed as a simple occupational hazard, much like overstock in a regular retail business. Eventually, the prostitute becomes stabilized in her calling, finds her friends almost exclusively in this type of industry, and acquires a recognized status as a prostitute.

The Call Girl

In the upper echelons of prostitution is the call girl who usually maintains her own apartment and keeps a book, in which she lists the names and phone numbers of her clients. Generally, she responds to calls, although she may also use her book of names to solicit. Most of the call girls encountered by the police have a deep hatred for men, demonstrate a pattern of lesbianism, and have very strong suicidal tendencies. Additionally, most of these women are characterized by having been rejected by both parents or they have a history of being sexually abused, sometimes prostitution is used as an attempt to replace affection that was missing during childhood.

In the 1990s, the typical call girl is equipped not only with a residence from which to operate, but also with a beeper and cellular phone. The call girl usually escalates to this level after working for a short time as a street walker. However, it should be noted that not many street walkers make it to call girl status. It takes a special kind of woman to elevate herself, gain enough money to go out on her own, and operate this way without being attached to pimps who dominate her. In effect, they have the same spirit of entrepreneurship as do persons who open up their own business.

The call girls we have encountered have ranged from the street walker who elevated herself to housewives and college students desiring to make extra money. Recently there was a call girl arrested in Princeton, New Jersey. It was later discovered that she was a police officer's wife operating out of her home. She had an appointment booked for one particular businessman when another steady client requested the exact same time. After she accidently divulged the name of the first client to the second client, there was an altercation involving these two gentlemen, which they both ultimately reported to the police. Of course, neither gentleman disclosed that they were clients of the woman, they simply stated that they had information that she was a prostitute. The police officer, who worked the four to twelve shift, never knew that his wife was out of the house, as every time he called her she answered the phone. She programmed her home phone to forward calls to her cellular phone so that she could pick up the phone wherever she went. She was home during the day when her husband was there but, while he was out on patrol, she was cruising the streets also, in a different type of business.

Massage Parlors

The massage parlor has come to be regarded as a type of illegal brothel and is often located within the neighborhood shopping district. Massage parlors are usually relatively inconspicuous. There's not much publicity or advertisement, and the outer facade of the building is not very ostentatious or enticing to the casual shopper. Frequently, these massage parlors advertise through small classified ads in local papers.

Police employ a method called the *duken* to close down massage parlors. The duken entails having a plainclothes police detective accost an unsuspecting victim about to enter the parlor. The officer will say something like, "We know who you are and what you are doing here, would you like your wife to find out about it?" Out of fear, the victim will introduce the officer to the employees of the massage parlor as a friend of his who wishes their services.

Once the detective gains entry, he plays the part of the customer coming in for the first time. The detective cannot carry a gun, identification cards, handcuffs or any object that would make the owner or employees of the massage parlor suspicious. Like the other patrons the officer then receives a massage.

Smart prostitution houses always tell their clients to go into a room, remove all their clothes, and wait for their girl. This is because most police departments will not allow their officers to remove their underwear when investigating houses of prostitution. And of course these prostitutes know all about this!

At no time may the detective suggest anything of a sexual nature to the masseuse. There must only be solicitation on the woman's part. The masseuse might attempt to sexually arouse the client while massaging his genitals, but at this point there is absolutely no cause for arrest. As an enticement to get involved in sexual intercourse or oral sex many of these massage parlors will have televisions showing X-rated movies. Only after the masseuse suggests sexual intercourse or oral sex and states a monetary fee is she liable for arrest. At this time the officer may make an arrest even though no actual intercourse or oral sex took place. Massage parlors usually employ only a few women as masseuses. Approximately two women do the massaging and soliciting. Their ages range from the mid-twenties to the mid-forties.

The Drug Addict Prostitute

A relatively recent addition to the world of prostitution, particularly in the United States, is the drug-addicted prostitute. Like the male drug addict, the female addict finds that after a time she must turn to an illegal activity to support her expensive drug habit. As males turn to burglary and robbery, women turn to prostitution.

A large percentage of street walkers are addicts. Call girls are not generally addicted. It is estimated that 90 percent of female addicts engage in prostitution at one time or another because prostitution is a quick source of the funds necessary to support their drug habit and the drug habits of the men with whom they live.

The Male Prostitute

In many large cities, particularly New York, male prostitutes have emerged as street walkers competing not for the needs of women seeking men, of course, but for the needs of men seeking men. Unfortunately, these male street walkers are young boys called *chicken hawks*, sometimes as young as nine or ten. These boys are the throwaway, disposable children of this century. Faced with no way to survive other than selling their bodies, they cruise the streets along with other prostitutes.

You would expect that these boys would appeal to strange, deviant, weird, homosexual men, however, the opposite is true. As with regular female prostitution, many of the clients for these chicken hawks themselves are married and have children. It is a type of sexual fantasy that they, of course, cannot get within their homes unless they sexually abuse the male children.

Many male prostitutes dress to appeal to both types of johns. Males cross-dress as transvestites and appear to be female. Depending on the type of john, many of the boys are beaten or sometimes killed when the male client finds out in the middle of the sex act that the prostitute is actually male. These types of injury occur hundreds of times in New York City alone over the course of a year.

Prostitution and the Mob

Prostitution is and has always been one of the steady money makers of organized crime. However, the mob has denied any major interest in this field ever since 1936 when Charles "Lucky" Luciano was sent to prison by a crusading New York district attorney. Luciano's operation included over two hundred prostitutes housed in at least ten, four to six bedroom apartments. His neighborhood managers directed the women to locations where the business was heavier than usual on certain nights. His bookers transported them between neighborhoods to achieve the consumer appeal inherent in new faces of prostitutes. His collectors and housekeepers made certain the prostitutes turned over the agreed percentage of their earnings. His icemen paid off in the police stations and court rooms. His strong arm men or enforcers maintained discipline and settled disputes. His bail-bondsmen, attorneys and physicians administered to the needs of the enterprise handling an arrest or ill health. A linen firm, which Lucky had an interest in, supplied the towels and sheets for his prostitution business.

This enterprise was the first concrete example of wrap-around organized crime operations and it made a great deal of money. However, it was also a landmark case that revealed the need to insulate top men from the operations of a criminal enterprise. Luciano, who did not participate in the daily workings of any prostitution house, was convicted because detectives unearthed evidence of his operation of the business and used the theory of conspiracy to prove his guilt.

It should be noted that prostitutes are frequently excellent informants and are very cooperative in dealing with the police. Since they work on the street, they witness many things and encounter many men over the course of their employment. It is also a bit surprising to find how many men will tell these women secrets they have never told anybody in their life. These prostitutes, like bartenders, are willing to listen and they keep an ear out for anything that may be able to help them should they be arrested by the police.

In the movies and television some prostitutes are portrayed as warm, loving individuals who can be saved by the right man. This is totally fictional. Our experiences have found that most prostitutes have, by the age of eighteen, lived more in their lives than most women forty to fifty years of age. They are hardnosed businesswomen, know the streets, and know how to survive. Prostitutes are not easily swayed by emotion and sentiment. The longer a prostitute works the streets, the more she realizes that is all she will ever be.

Whether in brothels or in the streets, under bridges or in automobiles, prostitution remains at the bottom of the social scale. It is the most convenient sexual outlet for legions of strangers, perverts and physically repulsive people in our midst. It performs a role that no other institution performs. In view of the conditions and the continued historical presence of prostitution, it is highly unlikely that it will ever be eliminated as a vice in society.

There are several organizations actively engaged in efforts to protect prostitutes: COYOTE in San Francisco, which stands for Calling Off Your Old Tired Ethics; PONY, which stands for the Prostitutes of New York; PUMA, which stands for the Prostitutes Union of Massachusetts; and ASP, the Association of Seattle Prostitutes. Prostitution appears to be developing a higher profile.

T E N

Armed Robbery

Armed robbery occurs when a person commits a theft with the following elements: The offender uses force, causes injury to the victim, or puts the victim in fear of bodily injury by threats.

The Professional Armed Robber

The professional robber spends his career striving for ultimate success—the big payoff, a robbery that will earn him enough money so he can live comfortably for the rest of his life. Professional robbers look for establishments with large sums of money readily at hand and a low risk of getting caught. The professional, because he takes pride in his work, will also expect a certain amount of publicity associated with his robbery.

Planning

Let's walk through the steps. Prior to the Christmas holidays, the diamond exchanges stock up anticipating holiday gift-giving. A professional may try to find an insider in the diamond exchange to help him plan the robbery. The insider may be a salesperson who will be paid off for his cooperation. Sometimes, the robber himself may apply for a position and work at the diamond exchange while he plans the robbery. This puts the robber in the best position to learn critical information.

The following questions will need to be answered: What type of security system do they have? Does it have a perimeter alarm? Are there panic buttons? Is there video surveillance? What is the best time to rob the store, that is when will the most merchandise and cash be on hand? Where is the merchandise kept and how it is secured? Is it in a locked safe? Is the safe only open at certain times of the day? Is there more than one place where the merchandise is kept?

He will have to know what other security arrangements are on the premises, such as armed or unarmed security personnel, and the location and the efficiency of the local police department. Are there additional armed or unarmed security block watchers? The professional will also, through his insiders, determine how many customers are likely to be in the store at different times. He will also formulate a plan to fence the stolen merchandise into money.

Through his research, the professional determines that Friday morning will be the best time to commit his robbery. Very few, if any, customers will be in the store. The display cases will be stocked in anticipation of upcoming payday and weekend sales. He has determined how to deal with all security devices and the best time to hit the premises to avoid the police.

The professional has decided to have one partner to commit the robbery. To gain entry, he will have to be let in through the front door designed to control access to the store. He and his assistant will be well dressed so entry is no problem.

The Checklist

What separates the amateur from the professional is not only training but preparation. Most nonprofessional robbers commit crimes of opportunity. The professional studies the crime and arranges a checklist of equipment needed, weapons that will be carried, and a schedule for the robbery. The checklist will encompass the entire operation, and is used to assure that all participants know their assignments.

Armed robberies require equipment, including small caliber weapons or handguns, which are easy to conceal. Other equipment may include masks; gloves, either vinyl or leather; and collapsible bags for carrying the merchandise. Plastic heavy-duty trash bags are ideal because they are strong enough to carry the proceeds yet can be concealed easily.

One factor that is often overlooked is the climate and weather conditions. A group of men walking down the street with jackets and gloves in the middle of summer is quite obvious.

Getting in and Getting Out

The entry may be made by our robbers all at once or one at a time. If they enter one at a time, the first person in will be the advance scout, who will survey the activity inside. This initial survey verifies that there need be no changes to the original plan and that no additional security has been added. If the scout feels that the time is not right, he will alert the other team members with a prearranged gesture.

Once inside, they may or may not cover their faces with masks, but will almost always use gloves to evade identification through fingerprints left at the scene.

Employees and any customers are rounded up and contained. The robbers pull out heavy-duty plastic trash bags and assault the display cases. Prior scouting showed where the expensive jewelry is kept, and this is collected first. If there is time, they will make an attempt to enter and loot the safe. Upon completion of the robbery, our robbers will exit the same door they entered, and flee the area.

Transportation to and from the premises is important. Stolen vehicles may be used and dropped off at locations where the stolen items and team members will be transferred. It is not uncommon to have team members separate to avoid detection. The loot will be held by one person, if possible. In their flight, they will change vehicles frequently, along with directions of travel. They may even hand off the loot to make the chance of apprehension less likely. A meeting will be arranged where the loot will be sorted out and divided. In other cases, one person may be responsible for fencing the goods and dividing the monies received.

Bank Robberies

A professional bank robber can be a single person or a gang. The gang usually controls the crowd inside the bank while one member cleans out the teller stations. This is especially important in large banks where the customer traffic is substantial. Bank robbers know that the easy money is in the teller stations, all the action will take place in this area. Bank robbers rarely enter vaults because of the time that it takes.

The lone robber is more likely to go to just one teller. In a small branch he may attempt more than one teller by starting at the middle teller or one close to a wall, so that he can be sure no one sends a silent alarm. He can also watch for other customers or security personnel entering the bank.

Lone robbers sometimes reveal their weapons; others just make threats, verbally or by writing demands on the back of a deposit slip. The robber will walk up to a teller and request the money be placed in a bag that he supplies. After receiving his money, he will promptly leave and follow steps to escape in a manner similar to the one used by our jewel thief.

The professional, through surveillance, will examine exit routes, parking for his escape vehicle, video surveillance locations, and the location of the bank's teller stations. Once inside, he will make use of this surveillance by acting familiar with the surroundings. For example, he won't be startled when greeted at the door.

When robbing a bank, it is important to carry the proper equipment. In most single-person robberies, a weapon will not be shown, but the robber will threaten its use. The bag used to carry the money can be a plastic shopping bag, a gym bag or even coat pockets.

When several people are robbing a bank, weapons will be shown immediately to control the customers in case one is an off-duty police officer or other professional. If one of the customers plans to stop the robbery, he will know immediately that customers along with employees may be injured in the crossfire.

Once inside, the customers will be collected or asked to lie on the floor. Certain members of the group will either stand at the door, collect the money from the tellers, or watch over customers and employees. They will exit and leave much like the criminals we described in the jewelry store heist.

Remember back a few years ago, when banks installed bulletproof glass to separate the teller from the customer? In some banks it would reach the ceiling to prevent a would-be robber from attempting to leap over the glass into the teller areas while robbing the bank. Walk into a bank today and see if this security method is still used. In most cases, they have been removed, because desperate armed robbers would demand money from the tellers by threatening to kill customers. This security measure, even though it may have been a good idea, did not work for the banking industry.

Armored Car Robberies

Although strip-mall banking and check cashing stores are convenient, they are also more vulnerable, and a secure method of transporting monies to and from them is critical. The trend toward establishing these banks greatly increased the use of armored cars and the amounts of money they carry.

Professional and amateur robbers both know that more money will be obtained from the robbery of an armored car than a bank. An armored car could carry several million dollars while making its rounds, which is obviously enticing to a bank robber who is very lucky if he makes ten to fifteen thousand dollars by cleaning out the teller stations.

Because armored car robberies are more risky and much harder to carry out, since the guards are well-trained and well-armed, armored car robberies are usually more violent. The same pre-planning takes place and will include some type of insider information about the arrival of the vehicle and the first and last stops it makes. The first and last stops are important because, if the armored vehicle is delivering money, it will contain more at the beginning of the route. If the armored vehicle is making cash pickups, then the more pickups, the more money it will contain at the end of the route. Robbers want to attack when the armored car will have the most money.

The armored car usually contains three armed personnel—the driver, a passenger up front, and one person in the back of the truck. Their weaponry will vary with the cargo and the location of their clients. All guards carry some type of handgun and will be in uniform. Military-style shotguns or rifles may or may not be carried.

The procedures of the guards are usually consistent. The driver may or may not exit the vehicle depending on the amount of the transfer. If it is a substantial amount, the driver will stand between the rear of the armored car and the establishment. The passenger will transport the money, and the person sitting in the bed of the truck will remain inside and only open the door at the time of transfer. This arrangement insures that the only loss is the amount removed for transfer and not the complete contents of the truck. Robbers know that an armored car is most vulnerable during the transfer of money, so this is when they strike. Their weapons will be out and at the ready, so there is usually an exchange of gunfire. Innocent civilians are highly likely to become victims of the gunfire.

While stealing money during transfer will net an armored car robber more than a bank robber, the most money will be obtained by stopping the vehicle before deliveries or after pickups. One way to stop the truck is by stopping a van or moving truck suddenly in front of the armored vehicle. The sliding rear door opens and a number of armed personnel exit. The criminals shoot at the driver's and passenger's front windows, which softens the bulletproof glass, so that bullets can be fired through it to kill the driver and passenger. Then, the rest of the gang informs the guard in the back of the truck that they will blow up the vehicle if the doors are not opened.

Armored car robbers have a backup team of additional personnel standing by with another vehicle, just in case they are needed to stop the police. These thieves will flee in the same manner as other armed robbers.

The Amateur

The amateur robber may come from any walk of life and may have many motivations. He may be a hard-working individual who, in circumstances beyond his control, decides he needs quick cash. He could also be a person with a substance addiction that has grown beyond his financial means. He may be a teenager or gangbanger looking for excitement, power and easy money.

Amateur robbers will commit their crimes during seasons when it is customary to have large amounts of money in the house, such as Christmas or during summer vacation. They find targets by observing victims who wear expensive jewelry or clothing. They might even follow an expensive vehicle back to a residence, and then as the owners are getting out, force the victims at gun point into their home and rob them. These robbers carry materials, such as handcuffs, rope and duct tape, which will be used to secure the victims. But, we have worked only a few armed robberies in which the victims were bound.

The Down-on-His-Luck'er

Let's first discuss how a first-time, middle-class, down-on-his-luck armed robber goes about committing a crime. He goes to a neighborhood where no one knows him and looks for a convenience store, gas station, small bank or department store. There will be little or no planning, and a short time before the robbery, he will try to motivate himself to commit the crime. He enters the location, and if he has a gun, he will show it. If not, he will threaten that he has one, and demand the money.

He will be noticeably nervous, which may include voice and body trembling and profuse sweating. The attendant being robbed will notice strong, foul-smelling body odor and bad breath due to additional perspiration and a dry mouth brought on by fear and/or excitement. Sometimes, alcohol or a narcotic may be used for a calming effect or to obtain the nerve to commit the crime.

If the employee refuses to turn over any money, which he should not do, the amateur will usually flee without the money. If he gets his money, he leaves and in most cases returns home. For his getaway, he will park a few blocks away in his own vehicle and walk to and from the robbery. If he used a weapon, he will usually make no attempt to rid himself of it.

The Juvenile

When a teenager or young adult robs a location, it will most likely be in or near his neighborhood. This is because young adults rarely have their own transportation. He will usually be assisted by his friends, and there may be some pre-planning prior to the robbery. However, the pre-planning is sketchy at best and basically includes only the location and who will approach the employee. They may scout just prior to the robbery to determine the number of people in the store. Juveniles almost always arm themselves with a cheap small caliber handgun.

Juvenile robbers are often quite violent and their

crimes usually end with serious injury or death to either the victim or the robber. The robber may be killed if the owner has a weapon available. If a customer walks into the store during the robbery, or if shooting breaks out during the robbery, the customer will become involved. This type of robbery is very fast, and the loot is usually just the money in the cash register. Getaway is on foot or in a stolen vehicle parked and left running just outside the door.

The Desperate Drug Addict

The substance abuser, because of his need for quick money, will usually perform a robbery of opportunity when the circumstances are right. These circumstances may include an elderly person walking alone, a person walking in a secluded area, or a intoxicated victim. He will brandish or threaten to have a knife or a gun and demand the money. He leaves the scene on foot.

Gang-Bangers

Gang members, mostly of Asian gangs, place a prominent businessman under surveillance and follow him home or to his place of business. When the businessman is alone, they approach him and become violent and abusive towards him. They tie him up and demand money. Asians have a custom of keeping money in their homes and places of business during certain holidays for luck. These are ideal times for the armed robbers to strike. If this robbery takes place in the victim's home, they will threaten any other family members present with bodily harm if they refuse to comply with their demands. Some Asian businessmen do not use banks the way they should, and large amounts of cash will be available for thieves.

Other armed robberies by young aggressive street gangs often become violent. The street people will demand money at gunpoint or threaten to cut you with their knife. There have even been cases where a person was threatened with an IV syringe filled with HIV-positive blood. The victim is followed until he reaches a secluded location where the robbery can take place undetected. Common choices include exit and entry stairways to subways, subway platforms in the late night or early morning hours, deserted streets, or vehicles waiting for a light to change.

Automatic Teller Robberies

Since automatic teller machines (ATMs) are available twenty-four hours a day, seven days a week, they are a ready source of quick cash for armed robbers. Most bank machines have a daily withdrawal limit, so the stolen amounts are relatively small, $500 or less.

The armed robber will stake out an isolated ATM machine in the late evening or early morning hours. When the victim arrives, he is evaluated for his vulnerabilities. By this we mean is the victim alone, big in stature, or one who looks like he may put up a struggle? Is there traffic on the sidewalks and streets?

Some ATMs are enclosed with a self-locking door. The robber will wait until the victim starts his transaction, and by either pre-rigging the door, defeating the locking mechanism, or having a magnetic card himself, gain entry into the ATM area.

The victim will then be forced at gunpoint or knife point to withdraw the entire transaction limit, which will be stolen by our thief. The thief will then exit on foot from the scene. There have also been reported cases where the victim was kidnapped and held for a period of time so that a daily routine of stealing can be achieved.

Taxis

Taxi drivers are one of the primary, if not the main, victims of armed robbery. They have ready cash from fares, and neither taxi nor driver is equipped with any form of personal protection.

Some taxis have limited protection from semi-bullet-proof glass between the driver's and passenger's compartment, but this is easily defeated. Most drivers will not use the air conditioner to save money on fuel, so they leave the driver's side window open. When the robber gets out, he walks over to the driver and places either a knife or a gun against the victim and demands the money.

Another method is to be picked up in a good section

of the city and be taken as a fare to a secluded area where the taxi driver is then held up for his money. The robber will leave the vehicle on foot and flee the scene. The more violent robbers shoot and kill the taxi driver.

The method of armed robbery is amateurish and the choice of weapons of amateur robbers is slight, but the brutality and violence is great. The weapons of choice are those that are available. Saturday Night Specials or large razors and knives are often used.

Check Cashing Outlets

Check cashing outlets are found in low-income areas where people, for a variety of reasons, are unable to cash their checks at an ordinary bank. The amount of money in these places varies, but in certain periods, such as the beginning of the month when people receive their public assistance or Social Security check, a lot of cash is necessary to meet the demands. Patrons using these services pay a fee, usually a percentage of the value of the check or money order being cashed.

Check cashing outlets are generally well secured with strong bullet stops and pry-resistant glass partitions and walls. To gain entry into the teller station or vault, a series of steps must be taken. These security procedures are much like those taken by an astronaut returning from space. The criminal must go through a series of air locks, but, unlike those used by an astronaut, these security locks are designed to keep unauthorized persons from entering. They must pass through one door, which will be secured behind them, and after that door is secured, a visual check through a surveillance camera is made. Only authorized personnel will be let through the inside door.

These businesses are extremely difficult, but most profitable, to hold up. Because of the difficulties, successful robberies are aided by employee incompetency or inside assistance. The inside assistant will be to in some way defeat security devices, perhaps by leaving doors unlocked. The incompetency might be when an employee is hungry for his lunch, fails to follow security procedures, and instead of going from one secured location to another, he just leaves all doors open.

The method used to rob these stores involves first surveying the habits of the employees. Once this is done it may simply be a matter of standing by when the lunch boy makes his delivery.

Female Armed Robbers

Female armed robbers, both professional and amateur, are rare. The professional female armed robber is more likely to be part of a gang, and will handle inside surveillance or act as a distraction during the actual holdup.

Some distractions we know of are having a young child fall and cry uncontrollably, having loud arguments between a customer and a salesperson, pretending not to speak English, and intimidating employees. Other methods include undressing or even urinating on the floor. This last works extremely well in crowded businesses and banks, especially in suburban areas where people are more easily shocked. While these diversion tactics are going on, the other associates grab key personnel and force them to turn over the merchandise or money.

Women are particularly good at surveillance, because who is going to question an attractive shopper?

Terrorist groups attempting to raise their funds through armed robbery may also use women as part of their gang.

The amateur female armed robber is most often a prostitute who robs her john or who is a desperate substance abuser. The prostitute will have the john undress and get ready for the sex act. Once the john is undressed, the prostitute uses a knife or razor to rob him. His clothes are thrown out of a window or taken with her when she leaves, to slow the john if he plans to alert the authorities. All in all, the female armed robber is not as common as you might think from watching movies.

E L E V E N

SAFECRACKING AND LOCKPICKING

When a person attempts to gain entry into a building for the purpose of removing items from a safe, they will be faced with a number of obstacles. The more valuable the prize, the more precautions the owner will take in securing it. These precautions are designed to deter entry rather than secure the premises. Overcoming these obstacles separates the professional from the amateur. Any building, safe or property that has security measures, no matter how well designed, will not keep a motivated, well-trained individual from entering.

Surveillance

When the burglar chooses his target, he first conducts a survey of the premises, much like the armed robbers. This survey may be conducted by an insider or it will be done

Fences and Gates

High barbed-wire fences and gates are a common deterrent, and they can be diabolically constructed to foil the most ingenious thief. They may be doubled, that is, two fences set a certain distance apart. The barbed wire can be placed in a number of ways. Traditional barbed wire, which contains wire strands and, every few inches, a twist of sharpened wire, is used mainly at the top of the fencing in layers of three. If this layer is perpendicular to the fence itself, this is designed both to keep people in and to keep people out. If this layer is facing away from the property at a 45 degree angle, it is designed to stop people from climbing onto the property. If this barbed wire is angled toward the property at a 45 degree angle, it is designed to keep people in the property.

Fencing can be placed side by side. The first fence with the barbed-wire layering is either perpendicular or at a 45 degree angle facing in. The second fencing has its barbed-wire layer facing at a 45 degree angle toward the first fence. If the perpetrator gets through the first fence, he will be trapped between the first and the second fence. This is also known as a security pattern. Not only does this help to keep people out, but it will lock them in for easy apprehension.

If someone wants to ensure additional security for his property, he will use what is called razor wire, or ribbon wire. This is the wire that you see while watching the evening news: United Nations troops are standing at a checkpoint and on the ground you will see curly wire. This wire has a razor-sharp section. The theory behind this wire is that once you come in contact with it, it entangles you in such a way as to hold you in place. The more you struggle to free yourself, the more entangled you become. This wire will also cause severe injury. Razor wire is mainly used either on the ground, attached to the fence, or mounted on top of the fence and gate areas either perpendicular or at a 45 degree angle facing in toward or out away from the property.

The gates for these fences could be secured with either a chain and padlock or a lock requiring a key. Another mechanism for securing gates is a motor designed to open the gate either in or out or to slide it alongside the fence.

---

through deception. This deception is achieved by disguising oneself as a maintenance person or utility company worker. Large companies are always looking for maintenance employees because of the high turnover, so it may be fairly easy to gain access into a building to conduct a surveillance.

Uniforms, including police uniforms, are easily obtained through mail order catalogs and supply houses. Identification can either be forged or stolen and in some cases, purchased out of catalogs.

Security, no matter how tight, is always less during working hours. This was evident with the World Trade Center bombing. Mauro is a master at testing security procedures. He can talk his way through just about any circumstance and has never been denied access to any location. This includes military bases, law enforcement agencies, businesses, and into areas for employees only without identifying himself as law enforcement.

Another method of obtaining needed information on the security procedures of a building is to act as a prospective customer and question an employee about security procedures while acting concerned for your security. The salesperson will be glad to brag to you more than enough information to complete your task.

The whole purpose of this surveillance procedure, no matter how it is carried out, is to see if the difficulties involved justify the rewards.

Upon completing the surveillance, the burglar will decide what alarms there are, and how to disarm or avoid them. He will research into the mechanics of the alarms and practice on them so no mistakes will be made during the actual job.

Getting Inside the Property

On television and in movies, burglars dress in dark clothing and wear sneakers. This is actually pretty accurate because running and jumping is easier while wearing sneakers and the soft soles generate less noise while walking.

The burglar carries a tool kit with the tools he feels he may need to gain entry. Some of these tools will include long, strong, flathead screwdrivers for prying, steel pry bars, flashlights, chisels, small mallets, jacks, hacksaws, battery-powered drills and saws. Gloves are always worn and vary from medical latex to leather workman gloves. Ski masks are optional. More enterprising burglars will carry police scanners to monitor local police communications and a portable radio handset for communications from inside to a lookout.

If the gate is secured by a chain and padlock, the burglar will just cut the chain or the padlock itself with bolt cutters. This whole procedure will take under ten seconds. The only problem with gated areas is that they are usually well lit, can be seen from the road, and may be guarded.

An easier method is to simply take the bolt cutters to a secluded part along the fence and snip the soft metal holders that secure the fencing to the fence post. This accomplishes two things: entry can be gained by simply lifting the bottom of the fence up and sliding under and there are no visible signs that the fence has been tampered with unless you are standing inches away from the fence post.

Getting Inside the Building

Our clever burglar has entered through the fencing and has observed that the doors are steel-reinforced with locks designed to slow entry into the premises. The windows are protected by steel bars. Some protective bars are designed with an interior bar that spins. If one were to saw through them, you would reach the inner bar that will spin as the saw blade comes in contact with it, making it impossible to cut completely through the bar.

We have seen resourceful thieves use building jacks or vehicle jacks to open the bars. The jacks are placed between the bars and, by activating the jack, the bars are bent apart so that one could squeeze through. Another method of defeating these bars is to pry them off the window itself or attack and remove a piece of the building where the bars are attached.

The burglar will use a method of entry that will be easiest and have the least chance of detection. Climbing on a roof, cutting a small hole, and lowering oneself down not only defeats perimeter alarms but gives a view of the room before entering. Another method is breaking through an outside wall to gain entry.

The whole premise of gates, fences, barbed wire, steel-reinforced doors and windows is not to keep people from getting in but to slow them down and give the law enforcement community a chance for apprehension.

If the merchandise inside the building warrants it, there will be armed guards on a twenty-four hour basis. Guards vary from a night watchman with a flashlight who walks through the building hourly to an armed patrol watch. In some cases, guard dogs will be used in addition to human guards or alone inside the buildings and in the gated area. These guard dogs sometimes have their voice boxes removed to stop them from barking so that they can more easily sneak up on the intruder. However, someone entering a building can disable guard dogs by sedating, poisoning, or simply shooting them.

Inside the Building

Once inside the building, the burglar will encounter a number of obstacles: Additional fencing and gates, brick and concrete barriers, and additional steel reinforced doors. The doors would most likely have alarms along with motion detectors protecting the hallways.

Alarm Systems

A major obstacle the burglar must overcome is the means of detection. Detection is accomplished through visual sightings by guards, special alarm systems to show the presence of an entry, and video systems that may be manned or recorded for viewing at a later date.

The only problem with video recording is that the thief may locate and remove the videotape before leaving. This is true in both manned and unmanned video stations. Sometimes the recorders are not turned on or the tapes are used over and over and the quality of the recording is poor, making video systems useless to the owner.

Alarms can be activated through audio transmission, by touch or vibration, light or heat sensitivity, and motion within the room. Transmission of the alarm can be sent over regular telephone wires or by cellular transmission. These outgoing alarm signals can be transferred to a central alarm center, the area police department or the business owner's home.

Once the alarm is activated, an audio alarm may or may not sound in the building. In some of the cases we have worked on, we observed that if there was an audio alarm present, it was disconnected prior to activation, or smashed from its stand shortly after sounding.

Alarm systems are powered by an alternating current—the electricity that comes from the electric pole that powers your home. Good alarm systems usually have a direct current or battery-powered backup. The backup is an additional protection from power loss. This power loss can be from a problem at the electric company, from storms causing black outs, or from the burglar cutting the power off to the building. As soon as the AC power is disconnected, the DC power activates, continuing the protection.

Educated thieves know that one method of disabling an alarm is to discontinue electricity to the building which they intend to burglarize. Cutting the electrical wiring leading into the building is one method of doing this, but it is quite dangerous. A safer and more effective way is to remove the electric meter from the meter box. This is accomplished by cutting the banding wire, undoing the locking clip, removing the band and pulling the meter straight toward you to disconnect the power.

You still have to worry about the DC backup system but once you gain entry into the building and locate the alarm system, you can then cut the wires coming from the batteries to disable it. By disconnecting the batteries, the alarm has no power to operate. Most good alarm systems not only have an audible alarm, whether it is a siren or a bell, but they will also have the ability to call an outside agency to alert them to the intrusion. One way to stop the call to an agency is to find the telephone lines going into the building and cut them with a wire cutter. But if the building has a cellular backup, the call will still go out.

The merchandise our burglar is seeking will then be located in a safe. This safe may or may not be hidden from view. In some cases, there will be two safes, one in plain view and the other hidden. The reason for this is the thief will spend most of his time attempting to open the first safe and may be happy with the few trinkets located inside.

This two-safe method is a growing trend in residential buildings of wealthy people. We recently heard a story where a wealthy businessman had two safes installed in his home. One his wife was aware of and the other she was not. Unknown to the husband, the wife had installed a safe for herself. The reason for all this security is simple, the amateur will not attempt entry and the professional will be delayed and hopefully apprehended.

Safecracking

Safecracking is the glamorous profession among thieves. A lot of training and experience is needed to accomplish this task. We have personally been to quite a few burglaries where safes have been involved. In our combined law enforcement careers dealing with all types of safes from the small personal safe to large bank vaults, we have never run across a safe that has been cracked or opened without force. Don't get us wrong. It does happen, but in all the safes that we have worked on, brute force was used to open them. Very rarely do you hear about a safe being opened by someone turning the combination dial—unless it was an inside job and they knew the combination of the lock.

The outside surface of a safe is one of the most difficult from which to obtain any type of latent fingerprint impressions. The safe manufacturer coats the outside surface with a material that makes them more secure, but makes our job a lot harder. This coating is either a wrinkled surface paint or the metal itself is indented. Safe industry people tell us they do this because it makes the outside of the safe more durable to nicks and scratches.

The first and easiest way to gain entry into a safe is, if the safe is small enough, to remove it from the premises where it can be worked on without worry of detection. Safes are designed to be placed in floors, walls and vaults. In vault types, it may be easier to gain entry by attacking the perimeter walls rather than the door of the safe. You would be surprised at how much time and expertise that goes into the vault door only to have the walls of the safe built of simple wallboard and 2×4s. This often happens in strip mall banks.

If you are going to attempt to gain entry by unlocking the safe, you will need to take with you a number of tools. You will need a heavy bag, preferably canvas or nylon to carry the tools. You will need flashlights to light the way, at least one that is the kind that you wear around your head to keep your hands free. Chisels, pry bars and hammers are also needed to assist you in forcing your way to your goal. Screwdrivers, needle-nosed pliers, battery-powered drills and saws will also be needed. A set of lock picking tools may also come in handy.

One tool for our high-tech thieves will be an amplifier microphone, which is placed on the safe door near the dial. By turning the dial left and then right or left depending on the safe, you can hear distinctive clicks as the inner mechanisms are engaged. These clicks are counted and translated into the numbers on the dial and then the safe can be opened.

Drilling the lock is another alternative. This is accomplished by first locating where the bolt hits home. You will use your amplifying microphone and open and close the handle quickly while moving the microphone around to determine where the bolt is located. You drill in this location and with any luck, the safe will open.

This bolt area on modern safes has reinforcement plates where a drill will not penetrate. One method of dealing with this problem is by preheating the area with a torch, letting it cool down, drilling a while and then heating the area again. Repeat this process until entry is gained.

When all else fails you may have to punch the safe. This method consists of striking the dial on the safe door hard with a large hammer to tear this dial off. Once you have done this your next step is to take a steel hole punch and try to punch out the center spindle. In some cases, this will allow the safe to open.

High-speed saws or grinders with carbon blades can be used to cut around or through locking mechanisms. Acetylene torches can also be used to cut into the safe, but care must be taken so as not to destroy the contents of the safe.

You may have realized that all this banging, sawing and drilling will make a lot of noise, so care must be taken to secure a location where the noise will not be heard and reported to the police. We have never come across any methods of sound suppression which is why the location of the theft is important. For example, you are not going to force open a safe on a main residential street in the summertime with all the windows of neighboring houses opened.

The safe door is the strongest point of a small safe. By turning a small safe upside down, you can often use a sledgehammer and chisel or a pick and axe and, by brute force, smash a hole into the bottom of the safe.

If you drill a small hole in one corner of the safe door, thereby missing all of the extra anti-theft protection, you may be able to peel back the layer of steel exposing any locking mechanisms. This peeling is accomplished with a pry bar, chisel and hammer.

To make certain that the safe contains valuable items, you may first want to go on a scouting expedition. This is accomplished by drilling a small hole into one of the walls of the safe and inserting a small video camera with a light unit to illuminate the contents of the safe.

Some safes contain additional security devices, such as alarms or so-called bait packs. Bait packs are designed to explode and release a tear gas and dye stain when you remove them. The tear gas is used to slow the getaway and the dye stain is to contaminate the valuables as well as mark the safecracker. This dye stain cannot be washed off the proceeds and will remain on a person for quite a while.

As we stated earlier, most of the safes we have encountered were opened by sheer force. The amateur will spend a great deal of time attacking the hinges on the door to gain entry. This attempt is totally useless because the locking bars that go through the safe door into the safe walls maintain the seal and integrity of the door. The only function of the hinges is to hold the door onto the safe when the door is opened or closed.

We believe that a criminal feels it is a lot easier to perform an armed robbery than to go through all the trouble and physical labor required to open a safe.

Our criminal, after going through one hell of an exhausting night, is resting comfortably in his own bed with the proceeds safely tucked underneath the mattress. The next thing he realizes is the police crashing through his door and arresting him. You ask how they got him so quickly? Well, he left his wallet at the scene and because he was so exhausted with all that physical labor, he forgot it.

Lockpicking

Picking a lock is not as easy as it looks on television and in the movies. While it is true that one can open some door locks with a credit card, most locks are much more complex. The common locks found in doors, cars, desks, filing cabinets and some small safes have what are known as pin tumbler locks. These locks offer a medium level of security protection.

Pin tumbler locks contain a series of small pins. These are the tumblers, held in place by other pins, which are called drivers, and the drivers are held in place by a series of springs. When the key for that lock is inserted, all the tumblers are driven to a certain point. This point allows the key to turn and the lock to unlock. The better the lock, the higher degree of tolerance that is needed between the key and the lock contacts. The degree of tolerance is how snugly the key must rest against the tumblers.

Pin tumbler locks are ones that can be picked. But a good portion of the time, the locks are stronger than the door, and therefore the door will be smashed to gain entry. On doors that are installed improperly, that is, with hinges exposed, the hinge pins will be removed, and the door will then be opened from the hinge side.

Lock experts, both legitimate and criminal, state that lockpickers must have a certain degree of dexterity. If you are clumsy and don't work well with your fingers, you will never become a lockpicker. To pick a lock one must practice, practice and practice some more. Well-made key locks require more talent than key locks that are found on desk and file cabinets.

One practices this craft by purchasing or, better yet, stealing the locks. Once these locks are obtained, our crooks practice until they get it right. When they are proficient, a door lock can be picked in as little as seven seconds. The whole key to this is putting just the right amount of pressure on the tumblers.

Before we describe how locks are picked, let's give you an inside tip on what burglars do to give them more time to escape when you arrive home a little earlier than planned. They place small pieces of broken toothpicks in the keyhole after they enter. The reason for this is your key will not fit into the lock, so you cannot enter your home. The noise that you make trying to open your door will alert our burglar that you are home.

If you were to pick a lock trying to maintain a degree of silence, you would use two items. The first item is a pick, which comes in a variety of sizes and shapes and is made from spring steel. Picks are either homemade or can be ordered from a catalog. The purchased picks are a lot better because they give you more variety. Picks are straight, curved or have different shapes cut into them. Obviously, the greater variety of picks, the greater versatility in the locks you can pick.

The second tool is a tension tool. The tension tool also comes in a variety of shapes and is made from spring steel. The tool is used to control pressure on the lock during the whole procedure. The tension tool will be turned in the direction the lock opens. We all have seen our special secret agent in the movies picking a lock with just one simple tool. This cannot be done, you need both the pick and tension tool. The tension tool is sometimes referred to as a tension wrench. This tension wrench keeps tension on the cylinder and assists in turning it to open the lock.

To review, the pick is slid into the key hole. It is manipulated to raise the pins to their opening point. The tension tool is directly below the pick and keeps pressure on the pins while rotating. The pressure that the tension tool causes holds the pins in their open position. The lockpicker feels the vibration of the pins in his fingers and hears a distinctive click.

Other items can be substituted for the pick and tension tool. The tension tool can be made from a strong steel wire with the tip bent slightly or perhaps a small jeweler's flathead screwdriver, again with the tip altered. The pick can be made with strong safety pins with the end sanded smooth. The one good thing about using a safety pin pick is that it could be easily hidden and looks harmless if located.

There are techniques to pick just about any lock made today. Locks that have been picked can be identified after examination at a forensics laboratory.

Some locks cannot be opened by picking. These locks have what is known as high-security pin tumblers. These pin tumblers are designed to discourage lockpicking. When you are attempting to open the lock these pin tumblers feel like they are at the open position when they are nowhere near that position.

Only the most skilled professional can open high-security locks by picking. Another method of entry requires taking a small high-speed hand drill and drilling a small hole just above the center of the tumblers. When this has been accomplished, the center of the lock will turn and the lock will open.

Another method similar to using a credit card, is to slip a small bent piece of wire through an opening in the door and attempt to unlock the lock from the inside. This is mainly done when you have a key entry on the outside of the door and a turning knob on the inside of the door. A thief can look through a window on the door, guide the bent wire onto the knob and turn it to open the lock. This is also a technique used to gain entry into vehicles.

A small screwdriver or pry bar can be inserted into the small opening between the frame and the door, and with minimal force, the door can be popped open. If the lock is an inexpensive one, two simple paper clips, opened and bent at 45 degree angles, can be placed horizontally one above the other. Jiggling the paper clips and turning the knob at the same time may be all that is needed to open the door.

One of the most widely used writer's gimmicks is the impression method. A person holds a piece of moldable wax or clay and the key is pressed into this material, forming an impression of the key, which can be easily duplicated. An important item to remember is that a key has two sides and both sides must have impressions.

When it comes to padlocks, the easiest method is just to cut the shackle, which is the curved part, with a bolt cutter.

Some interesting points to remember in lockpicking are that after you pick the lock open, you have to return it to normal or the key may not work properly which would cause detection. To determine which way to turn the tension tool, try it in one direction and, if that doesn't work, just use the tension tool in the opposite direction.

If your lockpicking is not going as swiftly as you would like, and your hands start to cramp, your picking will be unsuccessful. Take a moment to relax your hands and then go back to it.

If one does not possess the skill to pick locks, there are pick guns. They come in all shapes and sizes and are quite expensive. They are hard to conceal on your person and the law enforcement community will recognize them immediately.

To use a pick gun, you insert it into the key hole and lightly squeeze the trigger. The gun applies pressure in the same way as the tension tool and aligns the pins so that they are in the open position. Some pick guns will turn the knob, others you have to turn with a tension tool.

If all else fails, you can have your burglars break a window, reach inside and unlock the door.

T W E L V E

SMUGGLING

Leaders of narcotic trafficking networks are people who conspire with others to become the administrator or financier of an organization designed to profit from the unlawful manufacture, transport and distribution of a controlled substance. A drug lord can head up a major cartel employing hundreds of people or a small group. Smuggling is conducted worldwide, and they will use any scheme necessary to import their products.

Let's go into detail about the different types of drugs that are currently being smuggled.

Cocaine

In the 1800s, cocaine was legal in the United States. It was treated much like caffeine is today, and was used in a number of food products. The Harrison Anti-Narcotics Act, passed by Congress in 1914, outlawed possession of cocaine. Cocaine increased in popularity in the United States during the 1970s. At that time people believed that cocaine was not addictive, and this misconception made it the drug of choice.

Cocaine is grown in Colombia, Peru and other mountainous countries with suitable climates. Cocaine is extracted from the alkaloid of the leaves of the small coca bush. Cocaine increases energy and creates a feeling of confidence in the user; it is also a stimulant and will promote weight loss. These properties made cocaine popular with the Jet Set of the 1970s.

Drug smugglers remove the alkaloid through a series of dangerous procedures involving highly flammable chemicals. The end product is purified, which makes cocaine incredibly potent. Just about all exported cocaine is manufactured in the same area where it is grown. Cocaine is usually sold in grams or ounces packaged in small plastic bags. Additives such as inositol, baking soda and milk sugar are mixed with the cocaine until it is about fifty to seventy-five percent pure. Cocaine is *cut* this way to stretch the amount sold, bringing in more money.

Freebasing

Late in the 1970s and early in the 1980s, freebasing became the method of consumption of cocaine. Freebasing cocaine increases the potency of the drug. To freebase cocaine, the user mixes baking soda or sodium bicarbonate with the cocaine to remove the additives placed in it. The remaining cocaine is then placed into a pipe and a steady heat source from an open flame is applied to the pipe. This produces a vapor that is inhaled through the pipe directly into the lungs, causing an almost instantaneous reaction.

Crack

In the late 1980s, a new and more potent form of cocaine appeared on the inner-city streets. Crack is stronger, faster-acting and much cheaper than the powder form of cocaine. A piece of crack, which sells for around five dollars, is similar in shape and size to a peanut. Crack cocaine is very addictive, and one ounce of powder cocaine can make nearly 240 pieces of crack. Much like freebasing, crack is smoked through a pipe. When inhaled, this high-dose drug takes only seconds to show its effects. People using crack report that they became addicted after the first use. Crack is sold in small vials similar to perfume samplers. Crack is not only very addictive, but because of its purity, is also very toxic, and has a damaging effect on the nervous system.

Heroin

Heroin is once again increasing in popularity for two reasons: The price has gone down and the supply is plentiful. Heroin users feel that heroin is the safest of all the hard narcotics. Heroin is sold in glassine bags known as dime bags. A heroin addict can use as much as $600 a day in his habit. These glassine bags will have a stamped trademark, or legend, usually a name along with a picture. Some names seen on the streets are Tombstone, 44 Magnum, TNT and Minuteman. The heroin user will use these markings as a sort of consumers' guide for his product.

Heroin is either injected with a syringe under the skin, called skin popping, or directly into a vein, called mainlining. Smoking heroin is increasing in popularity because of the AIDS epidemic and a desire to avoid track marks. Track marks occur over time when the repetitive injections cause ulcering and collapsed veins.

Speedballs

Speedballs are a mixture of crack and heroin, which is generally smoked. Speedballs are like crack in many ways: It is a very intense, but short-lived, high, usually less than ten minutes.

Methamphetamine

The new kid on the block, which was first seen in Hawaii and sold by Filipino gangs, is called Ice. Ice is basically crystallized methamphetamine. Ice is almost 100 percent pure and is more lethal and addictive than any other drug. Ice resembles rock salt with different colors. These colors are used to determine the quality; the clearer the color, the better the quality. Ice is cheaper than cocaine or heroin and the effects have been known to last up to twenty-four hours. Ice, like crack, is very addictive and dangerous. Methods of ingestion are smoking, snorting or injection. Ice is predominantly a West Coast drug and is not seen much on the East Coast.

Designer Drugs

Designer drugs are manufactured to produce effects similar to other narcotic drugs. Designer drugs can be injected, smoked, snorted or come in a pill form. A person with a chemistry background produces designer drugs in small clandestine laboratories using no quality control. Some popular designer drugs are Fentanyl Citrate, referred to as China white, and Ecstasy, called Adam and XTC.

The Old Standbys

Hallucinogens were prevalent in the 1960s and are gaining popularity once again. LSD and PCP are two of the more well-known ones. They both have a number of street names. LSD is colorless and odorless, which makes it extremely dangerous. Some street names are Blotter Acid, Microdot and Orange Sunshine. PCP is a white crystal powder and when manufactured poorly, it could be tan or brown. Some street names for PCP are Angel Dust, Dust, Super Grass, Killer Weed, and Rocket Fuel. Hallucinogens are ingested by swallowing, and PCP is almost always smoked.

Marijuana was very popular during the 1960s and 1970s with the rock culture. It was widely used in the open. Marijuana decreased in popularity in the 1980s but is increasing in popularity once again. Marijuana is smoked either out of a pipe or in cigarette form.

Narcotics Street Value Price List

COCAINE

Quantity	*Price*
.10 gram (1/10)	$5-$20
.5 gram (½)	$25-$50
1.0 gram (1)	$40-$100
3.5 gram, ⅛ oz. (8-ball)	$125-$225
7.0 gram, ¼ oz. (quarter)	$250-$350
14.0 gram, ½ oz. (half)	$400-$600
28.8 gram, 1 oz.	$750-$1,200
125.0 gram, ⅛ kilo	$5,000-$7,500
444.0 gram, 1 pound	$12,000-$16,000
2.2 pounds, one kilo	$22,000
.1-.2 gram crack vials	$5-$20
Purity of cocaine	
.10 gram to ½ oz	25% to 75%
1 oz. to ⅛ kilo	25% to 50%
1 pound and above	70% pure
Crack cocaine	varies with supplier

HEROIN

Quantity	*Price*
.05 gram (dime bag)	$16-$20
Purity of heroin	
.05 gram	4% to 15%

METHAMPHETAMINE

Quantity	*Price*
one bag	$20-$25
½ gram	$40-$50
1 gram	$50-$100
⅛ ounce	$175-$250
½ ounce	$650-$750
1 ounce	$900-$1,400

MARIJUANA

Quantity	*Price*
joint	$1-$3
nickel bag	$5-$10
dime bag	$10-$20
one ounce	$150-$300
¼ pound	$300-$500
½ pound	$750-$1,500
1 pound	$1,400-$3,000
1 pound (semsemilla)	$2,400-$3,000

Asian Gangs

Opium is being grown in more places and the quality of heroin is becoming more pure, so the demand for heroin in the United States is increasing. Narcotics are smuggled in containers transported on ships. Most products that are shipped worldwide, are shipped in steel containers. But U.S. Customs lacks the manpower to check each and every container, so this is an ideal avenue for smuggling.

Asian gangs smuggle heroin by attaching a device to the bottom of a ship so that it will not be found if the ship is boarded by law enforcement authorities. Mother ships, like those used during prohibition, set anchor in international waters, small speed boats rendezvous with them, and the cargo is transferred. People are smuggled from China and other Asian countries to the United States in much the same way.

Asian gangs conceal their heroin inside of other objects: It may be inside cans of food, or stashed inside of statues, or just about anywhere. These people can be very creative!

The southeast Asian gangs are based in the Chinatowns of San Francisco and New York and mainly import and supply the heroin known as China White. Sometimes they are referred to as the Tongs, which was an organized crime group formed in nineteenth-century China. Enforcement is maintained by the Vietnamese gangs. The Asian traffickers smuggle from either coast, but the majority of the heroin is sold in the New York City area.

The Golden Triangle and Crescent

Because ports are open in the Middle East, the Golden Crescent is once again in business. Heroin processed in Afghanistan and Pakistan is finding its way through India, Iran and eventually Turkey. This area is known as the Middle Eastern heroin network, and some believe it is being run by the Syrians.

The Golden Triangle includes Hong Kong, Singapore, Laos, Burma, Taiwan and Thailand. Smuggling through these ports is easy because of the vast imports the United States receives from this area of the world.

The Asian region accounts for most of the narcotics smuggling, with Europe being next and South America and the Middle East at the end. Smuggling revenues are also used to support military operations in developing countries. For this reason, the never-ending supply of corrupt officials seems to make narcotic activity thrive.

Jamaican Criminal Groups

Jamaican organized crime groups are often referred to as posses. Like the Asian gangs, infiltration is next to impossible, because of the tight bonding and nationalities of the members. The posses have two main sources of revenue: narcotic smuggling and proficiency in providing false documentation. Posse groups are very violent and appreciate high-power, high-capacity weaponry. To kill their enemies, a single 9mm shot to the head or a drive-by shooting in a public place is popular. Other forms of killing by posses are disemboweling, mutilation and even beheading. Bodies are disposed of by dumping in remote sites. It is common to have a victim's body part sent to his family. Torture before killing is also commonplace.

The Colombians generally supply the posses with their merchandise. The posse flies the shipment by private aircraft from Colombia onto one of ninety illegal landing strips on the island of Jamaica. Jamaica is the ideal transfer point because it is so close to South America and the United States. All of these flights are arranged and cleared through the officials of the countries the plane flies over.

When landing in Jamaica, time of day is not important. The cargo is transferred from one plane to another, and the plane will then fly to its final destination, either Florida or Georgia to an unprotected landing strip. These planes are packed so full with narcotics that the pilot is totally enclosed and cannot exit the plane without first removing some of his cargo.

Posses import small amounts of narcotics using couriers and commercial airline flights. Young adults and females are popular couriers because they don't seem as suspicious. A female smuggler coming in from Jamaica once used a dead infant to smuggle the drugs—the body was cut open and the internal organs were removed and replaced with cocaine. The woman was apprehended when a suspicious crew member noticed the infant didn't move or cry. Marijuana and cocaine are smuggled in hidden spaces in carry-on luggage or body cavities. For larger loads, small private planes are loaded on municipal airports within the islands and transported to isolated landing strips in Florida. Posses also use cruise ships and smaller private boats for transportation.

Upon arriving with the contraband in the United States, posses usually lease vehicles, altered to sustain heavy loads. Many of these vehicles have sun roofs, which are used to fire weapons through when needed. Smuggling operations incorporate a caravan, using vehicles for transportation of the drugs and vehicles for protection, which carry personnel and weaponry.

Jamaican posses, like the Asian gangs, go to great lengths to protect their merchandise. All exits and entrances, windows and hallways of their strongholds are fortified to repel rapid entry by the police or rival drug gangs. These fortifications include hazardous traps, gunports and hidden compartments to hide their merchandise and weapons. The narcotic is not sold hand to hand, but through small holes in the door of their headquarters. Posses use money transfers, beepers and car telephones to conduct their business.

The Mob

Traditional organized crime families such as La Cosa Nostra are starting to expand into narcotics smuggling because most of the older members, who refused to take part in drug trafficking, are losing control due to assassinations and law enforcement efforts. The younger members are more violent risktakers and are more willing to smuggle for the fast money. La Cosa Nostra works out of the little Italy sections of large cities, such as New York and Philadelphia.

Black Gangs

Black gangs are very structured, organized crime units. At one time mostly located in Los Angeles County, over the last few years, black street gangs have emerged in inner cities throughout the United States. Currently, these gangs are increasing their activities in the Midwest. At present the narcotics they deal with are crack cocaine and phencyclidine (PCP).

The organization has no formal structure, but gangbangers selected to control the organization are chosen for several qualities. Physical appearance is important because one has to be able, if necessary, to use force to control any situation. A person's age is also important; the older the person, the more mature he will be in handling everyday problems. Arrest record and behavior also lead to a position of leadership.

The age of these enterprising young men is early twenties. As a gangbanger increases his fortune, he will tend not to get involved with the daily comings and goings of the gang. The gangbanger will support his gang by contributing large sums of money, weapons and narcotics.

As new recruits or members, gangbangers gain respect and power through behavior and displays of manhood, e.g. being brave, trustworthy, taking the rap, and going to jail. Recently, because of the money made through narcotics trafficking, prestige in the gang can also be obtained by making money in dealing drugs.

Gangs deal an enormous volume of drugs, which makes it possible to sell them more cheaply than their competition. Organized gangs are now dealing directly with the main suppliers of narcotics and are buying large quantities at one time. These purchases will be in the millions of dollars, and yes, it's all cash. Gangbangers who sell drugs are responsible for the narcotic itself and the money generated from its sale. If the total dollars don't reflect the sales, the gangbanger will suffer the consequences. The punishment will be proportionate to the amount of the loss. If the loss is large enough, it could get you killed.

Successful gangs purchase legitimate businesses to launder money and in an attempt to present a positive image to the community. They may even run for and win a political office. Some of the businesses gangbangers purchase are check cashing outlets, cellular phone and beeper companies, electronics stores, elite car washing services and parking garages. You can see how these types of businesses could be used for narcotic trafficking.

If the police put the heat on, gangbangers will generally move locations rather than look for trouble. This probably explains the recent spread to more rural areas. The gangs easily take over the new area, because they possess the heavy equipment necessary to overpower their rivals. They are heavily armed with assault weapons and semi-automatic handguns. They also have the muscle, the nerve, and the reputation, so rival drug gangs rarely put up a fight.

If gang members are arrested, they hire expensive attorneys to represent them and to deluge the area law enforcement community with bogus complaints and lawsuits.

Turkish Smugglers

Like other organized crime groups, Turkish heroin traders are almost all Turkish nationals. Turkish heroin smuggling is a family-owned small business that smuggles to relatives living in the United States. Turkish smugglers will also deal to Italian crime families. Heroin smuggled through Europe is transported in trucks that continue right into England. The truck is then loaded onto ship.

Istanbul, where most of the international flights from Turkey begin, is the center for the heroin smuggling. The drugs will flow from Istanbul, to Italy, Spain, Germany and the Baltic states. Because this flight pattern is well known, heroin smugglers use connecting flights from these countries to countries not known for narcotics smuggling. The Turkish smugglers hide their narcotics in hidden compartments in their clothes, carry-on luggage, cargo shipments and even mail. Sometimes, the narcotics will be smuggled in products, such as rugs or clothing made in the region.

Smuggling also occurs through small fishing ships and freighters. The small fishing vessels are accustomed to reporting to sea on a daily or weekly basis. While the small ships are out to sea, they will meet up with the larger sea-going freighters and the contraband will be transported from one ship to the other. These small fishing vessels will then return to shore and, either by disguising the contraband in their fish or by working during the night, remove the contraband.

Countries in Conflict

Pakistan, Afghanistan, India, Lebanon, West Africa and others all partially finance their struggles through the heroin trade. These countries, with the exception of Lebanon, smuggle heroin through a network of nationals and family members. Lebanon is assisted by Syria's.

Mexico is a substantial supplier of heroin used in the United States. This heroin is sometimes referred to as black tar, or brown tar, and is of very poor quality. Mexican smugglers bring their product across the border by truck or small private airplanes. Occasionally, the heroin will be hidden in products shipped to the United States.

Smuggling People into the U.S.

Whether it is for political or financial reasons or an attempt to flee law enforcement officials, people wish to leave their home country and emigrate to the United States. Asians, South Americans, Haitians and Africans comprise the primary influx of illegal aliens.

Most Asian—Chinese and Vietnamese—smugglers place large numbers of human cargo onto a small non-seaworthy ship and set sail for the United States. Ships have been located smuggling people to both coasts, and once in the United States, the people turn to prostitution and other illegal activities as a way to pay back the cost of transportation.

Mexico and South America create another nightmare for United States officials. Smugglers load up shipping trucks and attempt to elude officials by using little-known roads through the desert. This is very hazardous to the human cargo because they are sealed up in cramped quarters without proper ventilation or away to take care of basic human needs. The smugglers have been known to collect their fees and leave their cargo in the desert or even kill them.

Wealthy aliens seek out visas and other official papers needed to gain entry into the United States. Once inside, they reside in communities with their native people.

T H I R T E E N

SHOPLIFTERS

What type of people are shoplifting nowadays? Well, as you might expect, there are a large number of junkies who support their habit by shoplifting, but large numbers of professionals, housewives, teenagers, and people who have never before thought of stealing are turning to shoplifting.

As you may have guessed, the worse the economy and the higher the unemployment, the more shoplifting there is. Shoplifting is one of the few crimes directly related to the nation's economy. If someone does not have the money to pay for food because he's been laid off, he has to find a way to come home with what he did the week before. Some people will go out and get a job, some people will go out and get a second job, some people will do neither: Their primary job will be shoplifting. On the flip side, you would be surprised to know that many shoplifters, when caught, have more than enough money to pay for the items that they lifted.

Shoplifting: A Definition

Shoplifting is theft from the selling floor while a store is open for business. If an item is stolen from a storeroom in the back, that is burglary. If an employee steals merchandise or money from the store, that is internal theft. If a burglar or thief steals from another individual, that is robbery. Shoplifting, then, is defined as *larceny committed by the public*.

Reasons Why Amateurs Lift

In many cases a shoplifter sees something he or she desires greatly but does not have the money to buy. The items most susceptible to being stolen are those that are new on the market, because many people want the latest item, whether it be clothing or a home entertainment system. But they cannot afford it, so they shoplift it. They want to be cool, *now* not later.

Some shoplifters are the type of people who are shy, introverted and feel, in general, that no one respects them. Stealing is a power trip to them. By stealing and walking out of the store, they are in control of a situation. These people easily crumble under pressure and will cooperate fully when confronted with their crime.

Sad but true, many teenagers shoplift for one reason, to get the attention they lack at home. But how, you may ask, do they get attention if they are successful? Perhaps they leave the merchandise in a conspicuous place at home, hoping their parents will notice and question them about it. But, most likely, they will continue to shoplift until they are caught in the store. Mom or Dad must then come down to the store and rescue them.

Some psychologists believe that teenage shoplifting is a hostile act of defiance of authority and is an attempt to get back at their parents for something. This behavior may also be apparent in a husband or wife, who wishes to punish a domineering spouse.

Some people steal because they received poor service in the store. Many people who have been caught shoplifting picked out an item and first waited in line twenty minutes or more. After a long wait, they put the item in their bag or under their arm and left, thinking to themselves, "Well, if they want to make me wait twenty minutes to give them my money, they can just try and get me to pay for it."

Many shoplifters are older persons who are forced to live on a fixed income; their pension may have been enough years ago, but with today's prices, the money just won't go far. Trapped in this hopeless situation, they may turn to shoplifting.

Another interesting character who shoplifts is the person who does not actually need the item, who has plenty of money to pay for it, but believe it or not, they feel like their life is so boring they want to spice it up. Stealing is a game to them. If they can make their way out of the store with the item, they've won. It's kind of like chess, only sometimes they're checkmated and get caught.

The people described above are average amateur shoplifters. When they steal, they are usually alone and won't take anything other than what they need or desire.

The Professional Shoplifter

It doesn't take a whole lot of common sense to realize why the professional shoplifter steals: It's his livelihood. He makes his living by getting something for nothing. One thing you must remember about the professional shoplifter is that he or she seldom steals anything for himself. Whatever he takes he will sell or fence on the street. Most of the time, the professional shoplifter works by order. A person wants something and sends out some feelers to friends; a certain friend may reply that he can get it for him "wholesale." Most of the time the person who originally requested the item has no idea that his friend actually stole it.

Professional shoplifters are much like professional burglars in that they know exactly where everything is in the stores that they hit: security personnel, cameras, entrances and exits. They may spend days or weeks learning the layout of their targets. The professional shoplifter is experienced at this business and gets the job done quickly and cleanly. He often has a police record and may have organized crime connections who supply bail and get him out of jail, when needed.

The professional shoplifter will usually confine his efforts to a store located in an urban area. Even though the professional may not live in that area, he will pay to travel, because his bounty is tremendous. The greater density of people living in urban areas makes it much easier to unload the merchandise.

The Ideal Target

The professional shoplifter looks for stores with ideal conditions for theft. First, they select a medium to large store heavily stocked with merchandise. They will not select a small store because those are more easily supervised by security cameras and personnel. Additionally, believe it or not, a shoplifter likes a crowded store because there are more people in the aisles and more diversions for security personnel or clerks.

The worst thing a shoplifter can do is enter at the very beginning or very end of the day, because that is when the store is usually the least crowded and most filled with salespeople. In the morning management is usually present and the salespeople are milling around drinking coffee and waiting for customers to come in. At the end of the day, there is usually a manager on hand to count the take for the day, lock the store, and set the alarm, while other personnel are hanging around waiting for the store to close.

So, our perfect store is one that is medium to large with lots of traffic and located located in an urban area. Let's say the store is a K mart located in a major city in northern New Jersey. A professional shoplifting team may operate in many different ways.

The Diverson Technique

In the diversion technique the professional shoplifter, who already has been in the store many times and knows exactly where the merchandise is, will target a particular piece of merchandise. Let's say, the new Flowbee hair cutting systems, which are selling on television for $109.95. K mart has them in stock and on sale at $89.95. To take this merchandise out of the store the shoplifting team must be prepared to: (1) be able to steal the merchandise, and (2) be able to take the merchandise out of the store without being detected. Let's go down the aisle now, in K mart, where the Flowbees are stacked and follow the team as they operate, shall we?

The shoplifting team enters the store, usually separately. They walk down the aisle several times before they actually decide to perform the shoplifting. Sometimes a shoplifting team will be unable to steal the item they came for because of a clerk stocking merchandise or taking inventory on that aisle. The shoplifters will not hang around in the store, but will return at another time. Remember, these are professionals who rely on particular merchandise to pay their bills for the week, so they will not settle. If they came in for the Flowbees, they will not settle for shoelaces just to make a quick buck. They will come back at another time for the desired merchandise.

Let's presume that shoplifters #1 and #2, a team, have entered the store separately and have cased the aisle and found that there is absolutely no reason why they cannot steal the Flowbees today. Here is how they work the aisle:

1. Shoplifter #1 will bring a bag or some other bulky item into the store to carry the Flowbees out.
2. While shoplifter #1 is in the vicinity of the Flowbees, shoplifter #2 will create a diversion several aisles away.
3. There are so many diversions to choose from! Shoplifter #2 may shriek and fake a heart attack, so personnel from the store and other shoppers rush to her aid. She may accidentally knock over a large display, and again personnel from the store and other people will come to see what exactly happened. Or, believe it or not, shoplifter #2 may report to store personnel that she has located a shoplifter in an aisle very far away from shoplifter #1.

But remember that shoplifters #1 and #2 already know what the diversion is going to be, when it will occur and their cues. So let's say that shoplifter #2 has decided to knock over a large display of Captain Crunch, in aisle three, while the Flowbees are located in aisle six. As shoplifter #2 knocks this over, many people rush to see what happened. Shoplifter #1 quickly loads as many Flowbees into the shopping bag as possible and exits the store.

4. There is absolutely no reason why shoplifters #1 and #2 must leave the store together. So once shoplifter #1 is out of the store, and shoplifter #2 can't be charged with any crime, she can stay in the store as long as she wants. What usually happens is that shoplifter #2 stays in the store for a little while and scopes another item to be stolen. Of course, the next time the shoplifting team enters this particular store, they will try another diversionary tactic. They will also switch roles in the next shoplifting.

Nonstop Shop

Shoplifting teams simply walk up and down the aisles with large bags. They know where the security cameras are located from prior visits. They make sure that when they pick up the item with one hand it is quickly placed into the bag in front of them while the camera is behind them. You must see it to believe it. Many shoplifters will pick up an item from a shelf without breaking stride, place it in their bag, and keep walking around the aisles. Keep in mind that this is done while the shoplifter is walking quickly. They don't stop in the aisle or pick up the merchandise to look it over.

The quick pace prevents the security camera from picking up what has transpired, as many of the cameras have only black and white film of poor quality. Additionally, the shoplifters are relying on people to monitor these cameras in the store, and quite honestly, many security or clerical personnel do not monitor them. The cameras are hooked up to a VCR with a time lapse, which takes three to four second recordings from each camera in a zone.

The Drop-Off

Shoplifter #1 will be standing in a certain area, which is *not* in the area where the items will be stolen. Shoplifter #1 will be poised, however, looking at an item on a shelf and will have a large bag, somewhat open so that items can be easily placed into it, sitting on the floor. Shoplifter #2, who entered the store separately, will walk around the store and select the item that they both wish to steal. Shoplifter #2 walks around the store until he or she walks right behind shoplifter #1, and without breaking stride, drops that item into shoplifter #1's bag. This can be accomplished several different times at different locations in the store, because as long as shoplifter #1 and shoplifter #2 are not in the same location for any long period of time, they will not be suspected of being together.

The Junkie Drug Addict Shoplifter

The junkie drug addict shoplifter steals to support his drug habit. Junkies often work in pairs and sometimes in groups of three or four. A known shoplifting offender will appear in a store hoping to draw attention to himself, while his partner, who is probably not known to the police or store personnel, will actually make the lift. Once back on the street, they split the take after selling the items.

The shoplifting drug addict is very particular about what he or she steals. He knows that it is to his benefit to take items that have a very high resale value on the street. Each addict usually has his own specialty. In this way he becomes known to fences as the person to contact when a certain type of item is desired. Shirts and bras especially, but almost any article of clothing, are favorite items with junkies.

A very real and dangerous situation exists whenever a shoplifting junkie enters a store to steal. He may be so desperate for his next fix, and the need may make him so oblivious, that he may act rashly and with total disregard for other people's safety. The existence of the junkie shoplifter is one reason why all store personnel are warned to be extremely cautious in stopping shoplifters. If the shoplifter shows any sign of panic or of harming anybody, retail security people usually will be very happy with identifying the person and letting the police do the rest.

The Shoplifter Who Doesn't Shoplift

There he is, walking down the aisle. He's in the perfect location: A crowded large retail store in a crowded urban city. There he goes, turning down the aisle where all the electronic accessories are sold. He looks at a pair of small headphones that can easily be attached to a portable CD player. He looks at them, looks around, brazenly puts them underneath his jacket, and zips it up. He doesn't seem to care if somebody sees him as he walks down the aisle and turns the corner and heads right for the door! But just before he gets to the door, he takes the headphones from underneath his jacket and throws them under one of those large Rubbermaid recyclable trash cans on the bottom shelf of the rack. Why did he do this? Because he thought at the last minute he'd get caught? No, on the contrary, he wants to get caught and he wants to be accused of shoplifting, even though he has nothing in his hands. Why? Lawsuit.

If he convinces the store owner that he was falsely detained, and the police officer who responds that he is being falsely accused, he could get a couple of thousand dollars minimum for his "pain and suffering" and humiliation from being branded a shoplifter in front of all those people.

This type of shoplifter is on the rise because with lawsuits it is more advantageous for the shoplifter to pretend to take an item than to actually take it. These shoplifters are very well rehearsed. They case the store, just like any other professional, decide which item they want to pretend to shoplift, and focus on that item when they enter the store. But they also plan what is known as the ditch-off point, the point in the store where they are going to get rid of the item right before they get caught by the security personnel or an employee. This type of shoplifter waits longer for the payoff, but it's worth it!

Catching the Shoplifter

One of the common misconceptions is that a shoplifter has to actually leave the store before he can be apprehended by the police or security personnel. Many times the shoplifter feels that once he is past the doorway and out on the street, he has a chance of outrunning anybody who might choose to pursue him.

The laws vary in different states, but in many places security personnel may legally stop a shoplifting suspect once he leaves what is known as the paying area. The law provides that a retail store or its employees has the right to detain a suspected shoplifter. Detaining a person in a reasonable manner for a reasonable length of time is not an arrest and the shop will not be liable to the person detained. However, the store must notify the local police department as soon as possible.

In many states it is considered a theft to conceal goods on one's person while still inside the store. The shoplifter does not have to walk past the cash register to be eligible for apprehension in this scenario. In some states it may also be a crime to carry an item from one department to another within the same store, such as picking up an item in men's apparel and carrying it down to the lower level of the store where electronics are sold.

To apprehend the shoplifter successfully, the accuser, whether a security person or an employee of the store, has to prove one of the following elements:

1. He must prove that the theft was intentional. Sometimes intent can be extremely difficult to prove. Take the case of a woman shopper who slipped two scouring pads into her purse instead of her shopping cart. When the woman was prosecuted for shoplifting, her explanation was that she did not want the scouring pads to come in contact with the food in her cart, so she placed

them in her purse as a safety precaution. When she came to the checkout, she forgot to pay for them and left with them in her purse. In this particular incident, the court gave her the benefit of the doubt and dismissed the charges.

To prove intent, security people will allow the person to leave the store before they actually confront them. If the person passed the cash register without paying for his merchandise, it is usually quite easy to prove that the theft was intentional.

2. The shoplifter must actually have the article in his or her possession. Sometimes the shoplifter thinks that by dropping the item or throwing it away after he has been detected he can get out of the situation. But that is not the case if the store owner can prove that the person had possession.

3. The merchandise in question must be proved to be the property of the store and must be offered for sale. Through price tag codes and perhaps inventory sheets, the store owner can usually prove that the particular merchandise actually came from his store. But these things are not always as they seem.

   Let's take this scenario: A store security person observes an elderly woman look over a display of men's clothing. After a short while she rolls up a pair of men's trousers and hides them underneath her coat. Walking behind the display she then moves the trousers from under her coat to her shopping bag. She leaves the store. The security person, thinking that he as a clear-cut shoplifting case finds that no crime has been committed. Why? The lady could not speak or read any English as she was from Czechoslovakia. The woman wanted to buy her husband a pair of pants, just like the ones he likes so much, so she took his favorite pants to the store and compared them to make sure that she bought him the right thing. As she cannot speak or read English, she was too embarrassed to ask for help. Of course, cases like this are unique, but you can see how it behooves merchants (and their shoppers) to be able to easily identify their merchandise.

4. It must be proved that the shoplifter intended to use the stolen merchandise or to deprive the rightful owner of its use. Again, this is usually not to hard to prove, because if a person leaves the store or paying area with the merchandise he has hidden and avoided paying for, then of course he is depriving the rightful owner of its use. Store owners are getting pretty tough about shoplifting and the law is on their side.

FOURTEEN

WHITE COLLAR CRIME AND MONEY LAUNDERING

White Collar Crime is a catch-all phrase encompassing a variety of frauds, schemes and other nonviolent offenses. With more personal and professional business now being conducted electronically, it is easier for crooks to thrive at our expense. Home and car alarms are no longer adequate to protect us from becoming victims; these days we need security for our computers and credit cards as well.

Computers play as basic a roll in crime as they do in business and science. Computers are targets of thieves and as instruments of swindlers and intruders. Hackers pride themselves on gaining unauthorized access to data files. Money launderers cover the trails of dirty money, and common thieves can steal millions without leaving their desks. Their plundering can leave a crime scene empty of conventional clues. Only recently have states begun to pass laws that deal with computer crimes.

The annual loss from computer crime each year in the United States has been estimated as high as $100 billion. The average loss per incident can be as high as $600,000 compared to the average loss of $19,000 from all other kinds of thefts combined. The experts agree that computers will be the single greatest crime generator that we face in the future.

Telephones and Computers

Crimes involving the telecommunications industry have grown, especially since the break-up of the AT&T system. The Communications Fraud Control Association (CFCA) has estimated that phone companies lose as much as $500 million each year. The most common crime is the theft of long-distance access codes.

Fraudulent Telemarketing

Fraudulent telemarketing costs the industry about $200 million a year. You receive a card in the mail that says you won a prize and you need to call a particular number to claim it. These prizes can range anywhere from a new car to a "diamond" pendant. You call the company to redeem your prize, and they ask for your credit card number. You tell them that you want to know what prize you have won. They tell you that before they can tell you what prize you won, they need your credit card number to verify who you are. That's a fallacy in a couple of ways: (1) your credit card number isn't going to tell them who you are, only the banks have that information and banks do not reveal this information; and (2) most reputable companies do not do business this way. Now, there is a giant legitimate telemarketing industry out there. The problem occurs when you make the call or when you receive an unsolicited telephone call trying to get you to buy anything from land to travel packages, vitamins and water purification systems.

Travel. The travel industry, by and large, is legitimate and well run, but there are problems with postcards that say "you have won three days, four nights in Cancun or Florida or New Orleans, call this number." What they are trying to sell you is a $300 travel club membership. What they don't tell you is that you probably have to pay for plane fare to take a travel package to an exotic locale in the off-season. Or, they overbooked the hotel so the room will not be as nice as they described to you. They are going to sell you a lot less than what you think you are buying.

Scams seem to go in a cycle. As law enforcement tries to put these telemarketers out of business, they reappear through a method called *laundering*. The telemarketers go out to a small family business in a rural area that has come across hard times. They approach the owners with a way of bringing money into the business every week. All they want to do, they say, is use the business' merchant number to process credit card charges, and the telemarketers will give them a percentage. This seems like an easy way to make a couple thousand dollars a week, but when the people who purchased these items start calling and complaining about the product they received, the complaints fall back onto the small business owner. Their business will fail, and the bank will ultimately take the loss. We are starting to see more and more of this operation in Florida, Texas, California and the Midwest.

Computer Crimes

Individuals possessing modified personal ethics have long been at work devising methods to use the computer to satisfy greed. Money, physical assets, information, plans and virtually every other aspect of business entrusted to a computer have been stolen or otherwise criminally violated.

Losses can occur through criminal acts, malfunctions and natural disasters. Fraud, espionage and sabotage can be instigated by people, who may be employers, employees, suppliers, customers or other outsiders. Their intent may be personal gain or harm to the company. They may be interested in obtaining assets or information to establish or improve a competitive business. Finally, they may attempt to blackmail management with threats to perform criminal acts unless they are paid off.

What are the objects of computer crime? What attracts the criminal? Deliberate crimes against a company are always perpetrated for one or a combination of these three reasons: financial gain, competitive advantage or harm to the company.

Financial Fraud. Financial gains through fraud are perpetrated far more often than the other two. Many embezzlers have the attitude that "the company can afford it" or "the company will never miss it." The targets are money or property such as the computer itself or the company's products, services, information, marketing strategy or personnel records. Products and services are fenced for money, while information, marketing strategy or personnel records are sold to competitors or used for blackmail.

Payroll. Most sizable companies generate paychecks with the computer. Generally the information necessary to compute a payroll is stored in permanent computer files. This exposes the company in three ways: (1) Money can be stolen by manipulating the payroll; (2) These files can be sabotaged and are extremely costly to reconstruct; (3) Payroll information may be stolen and used to the detriment of the company.

Generally, tampering with payroll files can be made to appear accidental. If the criminal is discovered, he will plead accidental error and merely return the funds. Properly executed, the risk of prosecution in this type of theft is minimal.

In one case of payroll manipulation, a company submitted their payroll to a data processing center with a separate payroll report for each employee. The criminal simply inserted extra payroll reports into the system and removed them after the checks had been processed. Payroll checks were mailed to the nonexistent employees at a post office box from which the thief later retrieved them.

Accounts Receivable. The accounts receivable file can very well be the lifeblood of a company. It provides a reasonably complete listing of the company's customers, particularly the biggest ones, who would certainly be of interest to competitors. But most importantly, in many companies, the only records of money owed lies in the receivable file. If this file suddenly disappeared, could it be regenerated? Would the company be able to establish who owed what? If bills could not be sent out for a month or two and much of the monies owed were suddenly removed from the cash flow pipeline, could the company survive? A loss such as this could be fatal because the company is thrown on the mercy of its customers. Some pay, some don't. Bankruptcy is often the result.

Industrial Espionage. Computer crimes used to gain a competitive advantage are known as industrial espionage. Here the gain is the growth or increased profits of the competing company. Espionage is the practice of spying to obtain data or other information to gain unfair or dishonest advantages.

Operations Information. The marketing and sales files stored in a computer usually contain customer lists and sales records as well as compensation information for sales personnel. They could provide customer information and also reveal the salesmen who are most effective and the nature of their compensation plan. All this information will be of great interest to competitors.

Management information stored in a computer can also reveal many aspects of long-range operational planning. There is increased use of gaming techniques to predict the effectiveness of long-range options. The results of these studies often include a detailed performance analysis of various departments or divisions of the company. Such planning and gaming could be invaluable information to a competitor or supplier.

Sabotage. This is deliberate interference with the company's operation. Individuals perpetrating such crimes are usually looking for personal satisfaction such as settling a grudge rather than financial gain. Unions or activist groups may use sabotage to intimidate or blackmail management. Other activist groups may simply desire to draw public attention to a company whose activities are considered objectionable, unethical or illegal by these activists. An example of the groups might be anti-abortionists, environmentalists or animal rights activists.

Besides being susceptible to exploitation for financial gain, a data processing system is also susceptible to malicious damage, manipulation or destruction. The criminal may be an individual who feels he has not been given a fair deal by a company or it may be a striking labor union embroiled in negotiations with management. The intent here is to disrupt the company operations or blackmail the company by threatening such destruction.

At one time, Dow Chemical Company was a target of action groups opposing the Vietnam War. Its computer center was invaded and seriously damaged. The attackers had been thoroughly briefed; they understood the major points of vulnerability, and proceeded to effectively attack them. The cost to Dow was estimated at more than $1 million.

Banks and Financial Institutions. A small miscalculation of interest or service charges is generally not noticed by the customer. Multiplied by a large number of accounts, this small miscalculation can provide the criminal with a handsome annual bonus. From the institution's standpoint this type of embezzlement seldom raises suspicion until enough customers object. And, who really understands how that stuff is calculated? Most of us take it for granted that the interest on our bank statement is correct.

Borrowing funds, stocks or other assets is another form of fraud. For example: An accountant works for a firm handling a large corporation's account. He comes in over the weekend and transfers $30 to $40 million of a company's assets to his own personal account for a period of two days and then transfers them back on Sunday night, so it will not show up on Monday's posting. That employee can earn, over the course of a weekend, several hundred thousand dollars in interest.

We are aware of an individual who attempted this on one occasion, and as fate would have it, Murphy's Law ruled. While driving to the office late Sunday night to re-deposit the money back into the company's account, he was injured in a major accident and was hospitalized for three weeks. Needless to say when he left the hospital he went straight to the unemployment line!

Airline Reservation and Car Rental Systems. Since airline reservations and car rental systems rely heavily on data communications, wiretapping and other similar techniques can be used to obtain the information necessary to compromise the system. A terminal connection will provide access from which services can be obtained, after which the bills (computer records) may become lost (assigned to fictitious accounts) or fees reduced simply to nominal values. In the case of computerized car rental systems, an entire car's records can be shuffled through the agency until its auditing trail disappears. The entire car can then be made to disappear as well. In the case of airlines, baggage records are maintained on the main reservation file. Thus, it is possible to create a fictitious piece of baggage and then submit a claim for its loss.

Another computer scheme is *electronic data capture.* The way it works is you use a modem to manually enter credit card numbers. All you need is a list of numbers; you don't even need the card. Twenty-four hours later you have the money available to you and can draw out the money, leave town, and the local bank is left holding the bag. The bank wouldn't know about it until the customer gets his statement with the charge on it, which could be as much as forty-five days later, and reports that it's not their transaction. The charge reverts to the issuing bank and they are responsible for collecting the charge. This can cause serious losses for the banks.

Another fraud where the telephone and credit card are involved is *telephone sex.* Telephone sex operations are different from 900 numbers. The 900 numbers are typically billed by the telephone company. We're talking about a long-distance number you can call, and the first thing they want is a credit card number before they'll talk to you about anything you want to talk about. It's a booming business in different parts of the country. We get a lot of claims of fraud on the credit card. Typically the person talks two or three hours and then receives a bill with a charge of over $200. The customer will dispute the bill. A lot of the fraud comes when children get Mom and Dad's credit card number and call these services. There are also group sex calls, where people from different parts of the country, using their credit cards, can call and talk about whatever they want.

A new scheme that has popped up involves a disgruntled computer programmer who designs a program which dials into a credit card center. The computer will run a program designed to discover valid credit card numbers. The program inputs a series of credit card numbers that are submitted to the authorization center for a one dollar authorization. The center authorizes only the valid numbers. The programmer can take valid numbers and use them for other things, like ordering from catalogs.

Since mail order frauds can involve multiple states, government agencies have become involved in the investigations, including the Secret Service, the U.S. Attorney General's Office, and the Postal Inspections Service.

Money Laundering

Basically, money laundering is the conversion of money from a cash transaction system to a business transaction system. Money laundering involves hiding the paper trail that connects income to a person so he can evade the payment of taxes, avoid prosecution for federal, state or local offenses, and prevent any forfeiture of illegally derived income or assets.

It is estimated that $110 billion is laundered annually in the United States. This figure increases to $300 billion worldwide, which makes money laundering one of the most profitable businesses in the world. Intelligence sources indicate that a successful money laundering operation can launder an estimated $100 million or more annually.

It is clear that money laundering continues to pose a

significant financial threat to the United States, particularly the New York City metropolitan area. New York City faces money laundering at all three stages of the process: placement, layering and integration.

Placement *Where drug money is directly used to found an operation, such as a legitimate business.*

Layering *Where drug money is held or stockpiled while it is waiting to be integrated.*

Integration *Where illegal drug money is mingled with legitimate money, such as in a restaurant, gas station or conveneince store.*

The nature of the New York City metropolitan area offers unlimited opportunities for money laundering. New York is one of the world's largest seaports, the financial capital of the United States, contains two leading international airports, diverse ethnic populations and a high demand for illegal narcotics. The location of New York as a major international gateway together with a highly diverse international population make the city an especially attractive venue for money laundering.

New York City is the headquarters for six of the world's largest financial institutions (three of which are the influential securities markets), the five largest and most important commodities and futures exchanges, and eleven clearinghouse banks. As an important financial center, New York is in the center of enormous daily movements of money through wire transfers. Industry estimates indicate that between $900 billion and $1 trillion is moved daily through the New York City wire transfer systems. Those systems are believed to be a significant avenue for money launderers to move their illicit source monies; moreover, wire transfers have been increasingly used by money transmittal houses. A study conducted by United States Customs Service and New York Regional Intelligence Division pertaining to wire transfers concludes that wire transfers will continue to be a dominant means for money laundering and fraud.

Narcotics trafficking continues to thrive in the New York area. Statistics indicate that the New York City metropolitan area is an extremely large consumer market for all types of drugs. It is estimated that 50 percent of all heroin users and 16.6 percent of all cocaine abusers are located here. The ethnic diversity of New York City and the access to international transportation provide smuggling organizations with a hub for their smuggling and distribution of narcotics. With those activities comes the need to launder illicitly obtained proceeds.

Additional sources of information that may indicate potential money laundering trends or activity are the criminal referral reports (CRR) and suspicious transaction reports (STR). Bank officials file these forms with the government when, in their judgment, an unusual or suspicious transaction has taken place. A review of CRRs for the New York area over the past months has revealed that money laundering exists here.

The most common trend identified is *structuring*. Structuring is the act of making frequent multiple cash deposits, under $10,000, at one or more financial institutions with the intent to avoid the STR reporting requirements. Another red flag is when companies make deposits and/or withdrawals of unusually high sums of money not commensurate with their usual earnings or deposit and withdrawal patterns. Suspect wire transfer activity, primarily to overseas locations, has also been reported. It is not uncommon, especially in the inner cities, to find concentrations of specific nationalities or ethnic groups in particular neighborhoods or communities with ties to countries that export drugs.

Key Industries in Money Laundering Schemes

There are several industries that are particularly vulnerable to being used for money laundering activity. These tend to be cash intensive businesses that disguise large sums of illicit cash by mingling it with legitimate business proceeds. Bulk cash represents a problem for many criminals, especially drug dealers. Financial institutions used include banks, money transmitters and securities markets. The commercial business being used for money laundering includes the precious metals industry, travel agencies and both licensed and unlicensed couriers. Other cash intensive businesses such as liquor stores, automobile rental and convenience stores are also being used.

High-dollar retail businesses, such as exclusive clothiers, auto dealerships and high-volume cash businesses, such as service stations and convenience stores, are particularly vulnerable to use by money launderers. Criminals may use these businesses as legitimate sources of income or employment to justify large sums of cash or conspicuous material wealth. In some cases a seemingly legitimate business can serve as a base from which to operate illegally. As a laundering vehicle, seemingly legitimate companies can cloak the criminally derived profits as well as the identity of the owner of the illicit capital. Criminals can then establish new businesses for the purpose of laundering funds or they may attempt to corrupt an existing business.

The center of the diamond jewelry and precious metals industry for the United States is in New York City. The traditional secrecy and large amounts of money of this industry makes it particularly vulnerable to infiltration by money launderers. These industries have been the focus of three major drug money laundering indictments returned in the last five years.

The travel and transportation industries including freight forwarders and shipping companies are also particularly vulnerable to exploitation by money launderers.

Banks. We have found that a financial institution and its employees play a major role in money laundering activity, either wittingly or unwittingly. Investigations have disclosed that bank officers and other employees accepted bribes from criminals for receiving and processing large amounts of money without filing the appropriate government forms or by filing false reports. Numerous bank officials have been indicted for facilitating money laundering activities.

Wire transfers are believed to be a significant avenue for money launderers to move large sums of money. The Clearinghouse for Interbank Payer Systems (CHIPS) is located in New York City and handles over 90 percent of all United States dollar payments moving between countries around the world, including foreign trade payments and currency exchanges. Fedwire, the wire transfer system operated by the federal reserve, and the Society for Worldwide Interbank Financial Telecommunications (SWIFT) also conduct a substantial amount of wire transfer activity.

Securities Market. The Financial Securities Market is another area in which money laundering occurs. Our experience has shown that a good portion of all drug proceeds are laundered by this means. Currently, investigations in New York City indicate that drug dollars are being laundered through stocks and bonds. A recent study revealed the relative ease with which an investor can place currency into the system. This obviously means that some bank personnel are re-arranging the paperwork so that the proper forms are not being filed for deposits over ten thousand dollars.

Nonbank Financial Institutions. With the success of the Bank Secrecy Act (BSA), which requires all deposits of more than $10,000 be reported to the IRS, money launderers have begun to turn to alternatives other than the established traditional financial institutions. These alternative or nonbank institutions take the form of services labeled as money transmitters, check cashing services, courier services, travel agencies or currency exchange houses. The term *nonbank financial institution* has been used to loosely refer to:

1. Those persons or entities that receive money for the purpose of transmitting it, domestically or internationally, through courier, telegraph, computer networks, telex or facsimile.
2. Those persons or entities that convert money into traveler's checks or money orders from the currency of one country to the currency of another, and from personal checks, business checks, money orders or bank checks into currency.

These businesses or nonbanks have proliferated in recent years throughout the United States especially in densely populated areas and within the inner-city ethnic communities. These nonbanks are usually fairly diverse and provide services and opportunities that may assist the money launderer in creating anonymity: Little if any paper trails exist, and illicit funds are consolidated or co-mingled with legally gained funds or profits, thus concealing the true source or owner. These nonbanks may be operated independently in store fronts or within other businesses, such as liquor stores or travel agencies. These multifaceted establishments deal almost exclusively in cash received from the consumer in exchange for services.

Our knowledge of these types of launderers reveals that a substantial number of these nonbanks are active in the New York City area. Using a threshold of $100,000 in cash transactions reported via STRs over a two-year period, they produced approximately one hundred entities nationwide. Of these one hundred businesses, twenty-three, or about 25 percent, were located in the New York City area. A large portion of these were in Jackson Heights, Flushing and Queens. A majority of these New York businesses were owned by or employed ethnic groups such as Dominicans, Colombians, Haitians and Nigerians. Almost half of these businesses have been investigated by law enforcement, and some are suspected of or have been arrested for money laundering of cocaine trafficking proceeds.

Businesses operating as money transmitters are required to be licensed in the state of New York. These businesses are required to apply and post a bond to protect the consumer. The applications are subject to an investigation, which determines the suitability of the applicant. However, as best as we can determine, criminal background checks are not conducted. The number of unlicensed transmitters by far outweighs those businesses that are licensed by the state.

Jewelry and Precious Metals. The jewelry and precious metals industries (including diamonds and gold) for the

United States are centered in New York with wholesale dealers concentrated in the famous diamond district of Manhattan. The traditional secrecy and confidential business relationships surrounding these industries, the high value of the commodities, and the traditional cash nature of many transactions all combine to make these industries particularly vulnerable to money laundering activity. In fact, several law enforcement officials named the 42nd Street Diamond District as the single hottest spot in New York City for money laundering. The consensus was that no single ethnic group was involved but that almost all the legitimate businesses in the area had been approached by money launderers.

Some of the most important money laundering cases in New York involved these industries. The success of prosecutions involving hundreds of millions of dollars appears to have made a serious dent in the operations of these organizations. However, there is general agreement that outside of the financial industries the jewelry and precious metal industries continue to be the highest risk business for money laundering in New York and other states.

Retail Industry. An industry that is increasingly vulnerable to use by money launderers is the retail industry, specifically, high-dollar luxury stores that attract clients who have large sums of money. These clients have to launder or otherwise spend the money without attracting the attention of authorities, so they either make the purchases with cash or they enlist criminal associates or otherwise law-abiding citizens to make purchases. Retailers seduced by large cash payments, cash that they suspect came from illegal activity, feel that they have done nothing wrong or committed no crime when they accept this money. They fail to realize however, that the Money Laundering Control Act of 1986 expanded the definition of money laundering to make it illegal for people to accept cash knowing that it comes from illegal activities, especially if the deal itself is intended to hide the source of the money.

There sometimes exists an unholy alliance between

certain businesses and drug dealers that fuels the fire of drug trafficking. Some business strapped for cash are enticed by the opportunity for easy money, even if the cash has a dubious history. In some communities drug dealing is a career that people start while in their teens and childhood friendships between street kids often later turn into tempting situations for both the drug dealer and the legitimate retailer.

For the purposes of this discussion let's give a fictitious example of how an expensive clothing store, *John's Clothing Boutique*, in New York City might be used by money launderers.

John's is incorporated as J & A Inc., with two partners: John Linn and Adam Kurrocka. They deal primarily in imported Italian suits and shoes priced from $1,000 to $2,000. In reality Linn was selling thousands of dollars worth of clothes to the Raymond Edwards drug gang and to drug king pin Don Lewis through his New York Store. The narcotics traffickers purchased the expensive clothes with small bills and spent as much as $41,000 in a single day.

Linn began as a legitimate retailer, but the store was frequented by a childhood friend who had become one of New York City's biggest drug dealers. Linn eventually assisted the drug dealer in disposing of his illicit cash by selling him as much as $32,000 in clothes in one month, by purchasing luxury automobiles for the drug dealer registered in John's name, and by listing the criminal as an employee of the store. At the height of this partnership, the drug dealer and his associates spent as much as $457,995 at the store, and Linn registered, in his own name, six luxury cars, costing $234,371. All of this from a store that reported a total income of $85,600 during 1987 and 1988.

While Kurrocka, a master tailor from Turkey, escaped prosecution, Linn was recently convicted on thirty-four of sixty-seven counts of money laundering.

Convenience stores, liquor stores, restaurants and similar businesses are attractive to money launderers and provide an excellent legitimate cover. Since these are commonly cash heavy concerns, licit and illicit funds are easily co-mingled. Some drawbacks are that it requires the maintenance of a legitimate business, leaves an audit trail, filings have to be made with the state, county, and city and normal business records must be kept. And, there are limits to the amount of money that can be channeled through without attracting too much attention.

So how do these criminals operate? Someone with criminal intent has the option of either establishing a new business or purchasing an existing one. Money launderers will often seek out businesses under financial stress due to changing economic conditions. The purchase of an existing business is an advantage because the business pattern is already established and, as long as the business's cash flow does not dramatically shift, changes would not appear unusual. In any event the person attempting to use the business as a front for money laundering would tailor his activity to ensure that the business fits the norm and avoids attracting attention.

We cannot specifically state that a particular group or groups could be singled out for money laundering activities, and it could be that any ethnic group in an illegal activity could be involved. For example, Russian criminal groups are involved in gasoline tax and merchandise fraud as well as narcotics; Italian organized crime is involved in a myriad of criminal enterprises; Asian organized crime groups are involved in gambling and narcotics; and the criminal elements of the Dominican community are involved in narcotics. The Chinese as an ethnic group are not heavily involved in the drug trade, however, one Chinese group holds over 3,200 companies that have earned more than $1.3 billion yearly for the past seven years.

Money Orders

One way to launder money is to transfer currency into money orders. Money orders can be purchased from many different locations, not just banks—retail stores, pharmacies and post offices are just a few. Money orders can be made payable to anyone at any location worldwide. One can even list fictitious persons and addresses on these money orders, and have them cashed with little or no problem.

Narcotics dealers use the money orders mainly to reduce the volume of small denomination currency they receive in selling their wares. When a narcotics dealer sells his drugs on the street, most purchases are twenty dollars or less, which results in large piles of small bills. Drug dealers must relieve themselves of this currency and will do so by purchasing money orders.

If you have $1 million, all in twenties, you have fifty thousand twenty-dollar bills, a large bundle of money. By purchasing one thousand $1,000 money orders, you still have your million dollars, but you have dramatically reduced the bulk of the money. The only problem is that you need different people with different addresses to purchase one thousand money orders.

RICO

Congress enacted and passed the Racketeer Influenced and Corrupt Organizations statute, otherwise known as RICO, as Title IX of the Organized Crime Control Act of 1970. Congress wanted to have a way of controlling the money and power obtained from illegal activities, since these monies corrupt not only legal businesses, but aid in corruption of law enforcement. Congress also felt that organized crime became more powerful from the profits they received from their illegal activity.

RICO, since its earliest beginnings, has become the most controversial federal statute to date because first time criminals and small time dealers are losing their property and homes. Under RICO, racketeering activities cover any act or threat of act that involves murder, kidnapping, arson, extortion, robbery, gambling, bribery or narcotics. If a person receives any monetary gains from one of the prohibited activites, directly or not, they have violated RICO.

RICO allows the law enforcement community to confiscate any monies or properties obtained from gains made from illegal activities. It also provides for prison time and fines. These forfeited properties will be divided and shared through the various agencies involved in the arrest and prosecution of the criminal. In the early days of RICO, G-men drove around in seized luxury cars, but this is no longer a practice because it gave the government a bad public image.

Loan Sharking

Loan sharking is the lending of money at unusually high rates of interest. The victim is a person in serious financial straits. Loan sharking is considered one of the largest sources of revenue in organized crime next to gambling.

Loan sharking is a violation of laws regarding usury, that is, the lending of money at rates higher than those set by the government. Most loan sharking also involves extortion because of threats and violence used to obtain the loaned monies. The typical victim, short on credit and collateral and attempting to discharge a heavy short-term obligation, undertakes another more formidable financial burden through loansharks.

For each loan made by a loan shark, a pyramid of distributors or lenders exists. At each level a higher interest rate is used so that ultimately the customer is charged about 300 cents on the dollar per year. Ultimately, the million dollars laid out by the boss loan shark should generate half a million dollars in profit from myriad borrowers at the end of the year. The two objectives of the operation are the acquisition of money and the acquiring of legitimate business. To collect the payments due, loan sharks use *enforcement*, which is a term covering the truly criminal aspect of loan sharking, namely extortion. As a highly lucrative branch of organized crime, loan sharking is controlled by well-organized units each divided into about four levels of operating personnel and headed by a chief or boss.

The Boss Loan Shark is at the top of the unit and is a high-ranking person in the crime group. Although he may be the head of a legitimate business, such as a bank or mortgage company, his loan sharking operation is conducted without established headquarters. He provides the financing and the overall supervision of the operation. For example, in the beginning of the year he will distribute a million dollars among his ten lieutenants with the simple instructions: "It doesn't matter to me what you get for loaning out the money, but I want a certain percentage per week."

Lieutenants. The second level is held by ten lieutenants who distribute about a hundred thousand dollars among the subordinates with similar instructions requiring that they get slightly more percentage per week interest.

Subordinates. Each of the lieutenants has about thirty subordinates who may themselves do the lending, if the loan is large enough, or who may have their own subordinates who do the lending. Again the interest requirement will be slightly higher.

Bookmakers. The fourth level is where most of the actual lending is conducted. This may consist of working bookmakers and street corner hoodlums. The interest rate at this level is usually 5 percent of the principal per week and may be higher.

Since any successful business is based on sound business policy calculated to yield predictable results, so too has loan sharking developed a reliable procedure for dealing with default on the loan.

The first rule is that the lender makes the rules. Let's take a case where a business owner is given a $6,000 loan by a loan shark. The borrower, the businessman, made three payments and then missed two. As a penalty, the loan shark declared that the debt was now $12,000 with the 5 percent interest per week now on this larger sum. Again the businessman failed to pay and the declared principal was increased to $17,000. Finally when the debt had gone to $25,000 the debtor was called to account.

The loan shark then declared himself a half partner in the victim's business. Now he was to collect half of the business profits as well as the weekly payments on the old loan. Eventually the situation becomes hopeless and the loan shark states that his final offer is that "if you forget about the business we'll forget about the loan." The business is now the loan shark's!

A sit down occurs when it appears the victim is in serious trouble and can no longer meet the payments. This meeting is presided over by a recognized underworld chief who decides what lump sum the loan and the accumulated interest can be settled for. It is a court for which there is no appeal, of course.

Let's consider the case of a company whose chief executive received a loan of $22,000 with interest of $1,100 per week. Later another $6,500 was lent and the total interest payments became $1,425 per week without ever diminishing the amount owed. Soon the executive was convinced that he could not maintain the payments. Although he had already spent $25,000 in interest, he still owed the *entire* principal of the loan.

A sit down was called with the chief loan shark. It was ruled that the chief should take over the company and operate its plant. In a few months the company was looted of all its assets and driven into bankruptcy.

Failure to meet payments is met with grave disapproval and followed by the imposition of severe sanctions. Depending on the nature of the case and especially on the victim's assets, a decision is made and a penalty imposed. This penalty may take the form of assault, murder or appropriation of the customer's property.

Loan sharks are very successful because the police find them difficult to investigate. It is a personal transaction to which there are usually no witnesses other than the two persons involved. In fact, many loans are negotiated under circumstances the victim is actually reluctant to reveal. For example, gambling losses are a common cause of approaching a loan shark. A husband takes five hundred dollars from his paycheck and gambles it away. He finds that he owes the loan shark seven hundred dollars within twenty-four hours and will not want to admit to his spouse where the first five hundred actually went. This is the last type of person that will report to the police that he is a victim of loan sharking.

All states have statutes covering extortion and conspiracy in an attempt to control the criminal activities of loan sharks. However, in cases of loan sharking that *are* reported to the police, the only person arrested, indicted and sent to prison is the enforcer of the loan shark, who, when being sent to break a few arms and legs, was set up by the police. In these cases our experience has shown that the victim, even though he has gone to the police, will not be bothered any further. After all, why should the loan shark bother with a victim who is under police surveillance when the city is filled with customers ready, willing and able to pay 5 percent interest per week!

Index